Welcome to Washington

by Eugenia M. Horstman

Welcome to Washington. Published by Interpretive Publications, Inc., P.O. Box 1383, Flagstaff, Arizona 86002-1383. © 1981 Eugenia M. Horstman. Revised edition 1987. ISBN 0-936478-11-X.

THE CITY OF WASHINGTON

The story of the capital of the United States is inextricably entwined with the birth of the nation itself, so a brief review of certain events in U.S. history will help orient visitors to the city's major sightseeing attractions.

Until the late eighteenth century Americans were subject to the British Crown. But when British rule became more and more repressive, the colonies sent representatives to a First Continental Congress in Philadelphia, Pennsylvania, in 1774 and a Second Continental Congress in 1775 to decide on some concerted action they could take. When King George III refused to redress the colonists' grievances, the Continental Congress created a Continental Army and elected as its commander-in-chief George Washington, who had earlier distinguished himself as a military leader in the French and Indian War.

In 1776 Congress approved a Declaration of Independence and sent it to King George III. This document asserted the independence of the colonies from British rule. All who signed the document did so at the risk of their lives. If the American Revolution were unsuccessful, they would likely be hanged as traitors to the British Crown.

For the following five years the colonists fought for their freedom. From a small army of inadequately supplied, untrained recruits, George Washington forged an effective, maneuverable fighting force that finally won independence from the richest, most powerful empire in the world at that time. The colonists won the decisive military victory at Yorktown, Virginia, in 1781. The assistance of France was crucial to this success. Great Britain formally recognized the independence of the United States of America in 1783 by signing the Treaty of Paris.

George Washington's military success and personal character made him the hero of the new nation. When the Constitutional Convention met in 1787 to draft the Constitution of the United States, Washington was asked to preside. And in 1789 he was unanimously elected as the first president of the United States.

The following year the Congress decided to build a new city as the nation's capital, and it authorized President Washington to choose the location. He selected an area of sparsely inhabited farmland on the banks of the Potomac River that was centrally located in the thirteen new states and not far from the prosperous ports of Georgetown and Alexandria. The site was designated a federal district to make it politically separate from all states, and it was named "District of Columbia" after Christopher Columbus. The city was named after George Washington. President Washington and Secretary of State Thomas Jefferson engaged Pierre L'Enfant—French engineer and architect—to design the new city.

For ten years the government met in New York and Philadelphia while the Capitol and the White House were being built. In 1800 the government moved to Washington, D.C., but even then the Capitol and the White House were still incomplete. The city was no more than a shabby little village, with a population of about 3,000 and only 372 houses. Newspapers in other cities ridiculed it as "a city of streets without homes." And those streets were dirt, which became mud in rainy weather.

Washington, D.C., remained relatively small and parochial for half a century. Then the new nation was torn asunder by the trauma of Civil War beginning in 1861. Countryman fought countryman, and brother fought brother in a terrible four-year bloodbath that ended in 1865 when the South surrendered to the North.

The capital city began to grow after the end of the Civil War as rows of houses spread east and north. By the early 1870s the city's population had increased to 131,700, and such civic improvements as paved streets, utility systems, and horse-drawn public transportation made life more comfortable and convenient. Washington, D.C., finally began to take its place among the world's great capitals.

Today Washington, D.C., is one of the world's most beautiful cities. With broad, tree-lined avenues; spacious parks and commons, many with statuary or fountains; monumental public buildings; a rocky glen meandering through one corner; fine shops and restaurants; and a sophisticated international community, Washington is a cosmopolitan yet relaxed city of grace and dignity that you will enjoy exploring. Let's explore now the major visitor attractions, described generally in historical sequence.

The Mall sweeps westward from the Capitol toward the Monument and the Potomac River.

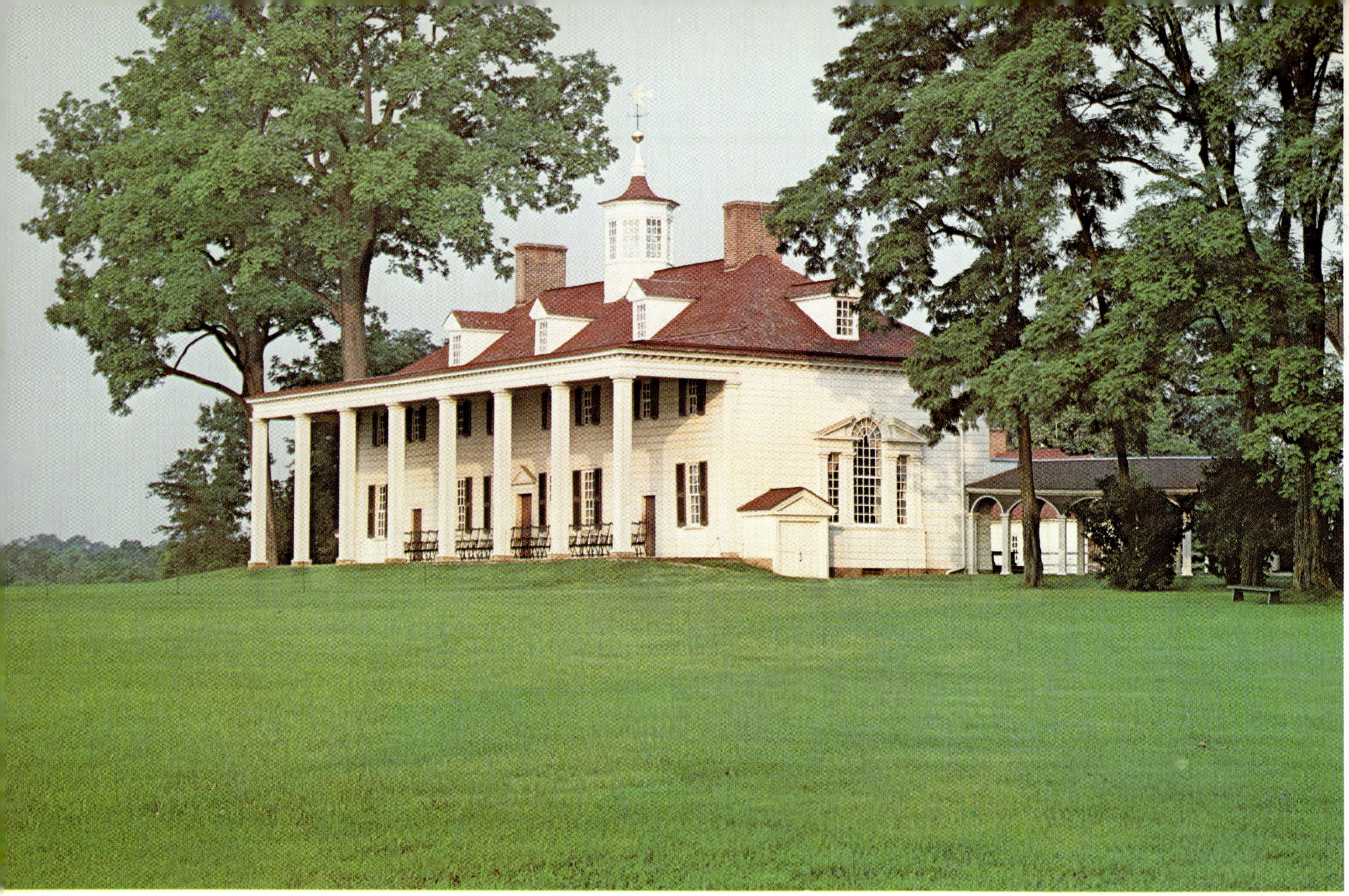

© Mount Vernon Ladies Association

© Mount Vernon Ladies Association

© Mount Vernon Ladies Association

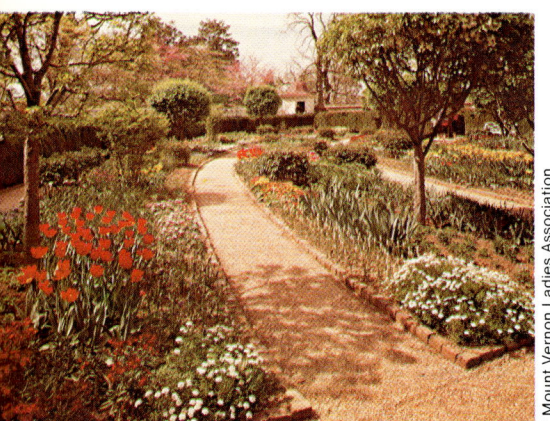

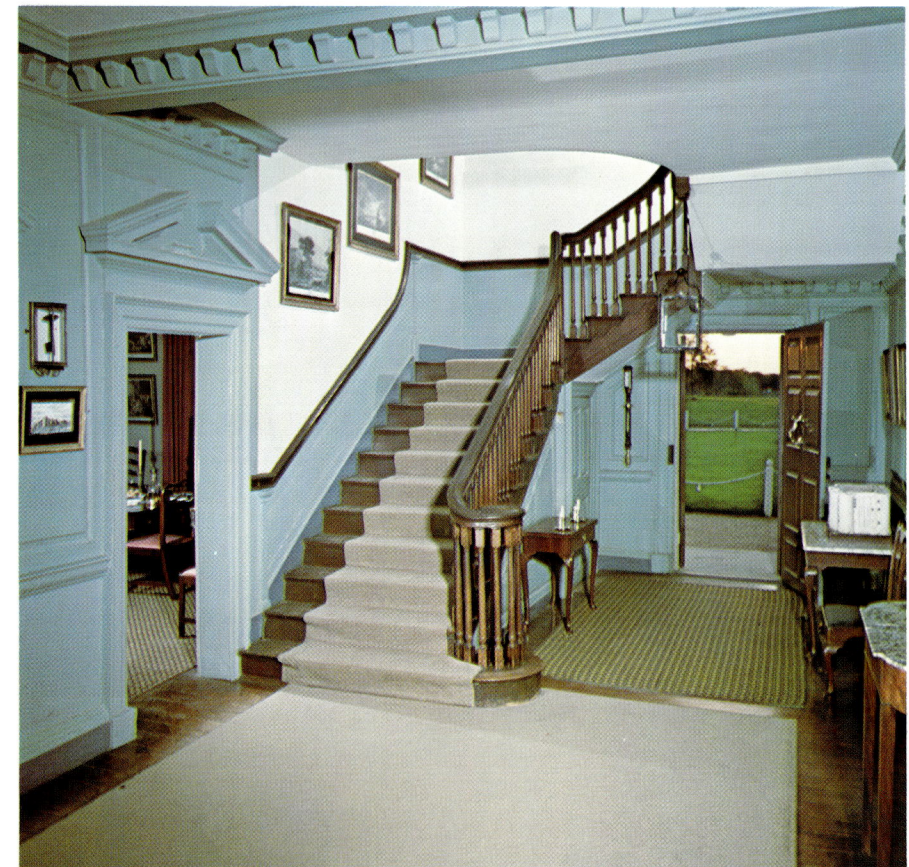

George Washington personally designed the landscaping of the grounds and the improvements to the buildings of his country estate. A key to the Bastille—a French prison liberated in the early days of the French Revolution—hangs on the wall in the center hall (at right). It was a gift from the Marquis de Lafayette, the French patriot who had served in the American Revolution with Washington and was instrumental in obtaining French aid for the Americans.

MOUNT VERNON

Whenever a ship of the U.S. Navy passes Mount Vernon, on the Virginia shore of the Potomac River, the flag is lowered to half-mast, the bell is tolled, and the crew stands at attention. This solemn ritual honors George Washington, who lies entombed here in a simple marble sarcophagus in the outer vault of a brick tomb.

Washington acquired Mount Vernon in 1754 at the age of 22 after his older brother died. From 1752 to 1759 Washington was engaged in military campaigns against the French and Indians, so he visited Mount Vernon infrequently. In 1759, at age 27, George married Martha Dandridge Custis, a young widow with two children—John Parke Custis and Martha Parke Custis. George and Martha never had children, but George reared his wife's children as his own. Later he reared two of his wife's grandchildren—"Nelly" Custis and George Washington Parke Custis—after their father, John Parke Custis, died.

The first sixteen years of marriage were the happiest in the Washingtons' lives. George divided his property into five farms, each with its own buildings, livestock, workers, and overseer. The four outlying farms were well-cultivated, productive farms; but Washington developed the Mansion House Farm as a country gentleman's estate. Actually, the plantation was a small, self-sufficient community. Some 90 people lived at the Mansion House Farm, and 150 more lived on the other four farms.

Every day Washington rode over his properties, inspecting, planning, and directing their operations. He personally designed the landscaping of the grounds and improvements to the buildings. Although he never left America, his estate is reminiscent of the grand country estates of England.

When the American Revolution erupted and Washington was commissioned as Commander-in-Chief of the Continental Army, a cousin managed the plantation while Washington was away at war. Martha stayed with her husband at his winter encampments for eight years, returning to Mount Vernon each spring when fighting resumed.

At the end of the war Washington returned to Mount Vernon to pursue his love of farming. But in 1787 he was called to preside over the convention that drafted the Constitution of the United States, and in 1789 he was elected as first president of the new nation.

During his 8-year term of office, the Washingtons lived in New York and Philadelphia. But Washington still took great personal interest in his country estate, and he directed farm operations by weekly correspondence. Finally he returned home in 1797, where he died two years later at the age of 67. Martha died 2½ years later.

Well situated on a high bluff, the mansion enjoys a sweeping vista of the Potomac River. A high-columned portico—a Washington innovation—dominates the river front of the house. The wooden siding of the house and outbuildings is another unusual feature. It was beveled to resemble stone blocks, and sand was applied to the wet paint to complete the effect. The house is approached from the west by a serpentine driveway on either side of the well-manicured bowling green.

Outbuildings flank the mansion around a courtyard. The kitchen garden is on the south side of the bowling green; the formal flower garden is on the north side. The magnificent, fragrant boxwood hedges in this garden were planted in 1785.

The Mount Vernon Ladies Association, a private group, has faithfully restored the Mansion House Farm to its original state. Original furnishings have been used when possible; period pieces have been substituted when originals could not be found. Strolling through the gardens or peeking into the parlor or the kitchen, you will begin to appreciate the industrious but simpler lifestyle of a vanished era. For Mount Vernon today is a prime example of an eighteenth century Virginia plantation manor—and a national shrine to the first great hero of the United States.

Mount Vernon, Virginia, 24 km (15 miles) south on George Washington Parkway. Admission fee. Facilities: Restrooms/Telephone/Restaurant/Parking/Accessible by wheelchair

THE WASHINGTON MONUMENT

When Britain formally recognized American independence in 1783 by signing the Treaty of Paris, the Continental Congress passed a resolution to erect an equestrian statue of Revolutionary War hero George Washington. Washington, however, objected to the expenditure of limited government funds on such a statue, so the project was dropped.

After Washington's death many proposals were advanced for the erection of a suitable memorial. A tomb was built in the Capitol building; but officials of the State of Virginia objected to removal of Washington's remains from Mount Vernon, so his body was left there. Nothing was done about a memorial until thirty-four years after Washington's death.

In 1883, influential citizens of the capital city organized the Washington National Monument Society to raise money by popular subscription to build a monument to George Washington. They decided against building an equestrian statue and instead selected a design in a general competition.

The site of L'Enfant's original location for the "equestrian statue" was selected, but it had to be moved 100 meters southeast to assure a better foundation for the great weight of the monument. The cornerstone was laid on Independence Day, July 4, 1848, using the same trowel Washington himself had used to lay the cornerstone of the Capitol building in 1793.

An ingenious means of promoting the project was devised. Building blocks as well as funds were solicited. Every state and territory of the United States donated carved memorial blocks. Stones carved with tributes to George Washington arrived from clubs, churches, labor and business organizations, professional societies, fire departments, and municipalities. The Cherokee Indian Nation donated a stone. China, Siam, Greece, Turkey, Switzerland, Wales, and Brazil sent blocks. Commodore Perry brought a tribute block from Japan when he returned from opening trade with that country in 1854. In all, 190 of these blocks were used to line the shaft, where visitors using the stairway could see them.

Lack of funding halted construction in 1854, and later the Civil War diverted attention from memorial-building. The Monument stood incomplete for nearly 25 years as a stub only 45.7 meters (150 feet) high.

After the Civil War Congress authorized funds to complete construction of the Monument, and the building was finally opened to the public in 1888.

The obelisk known locally as The Monument rises 169.3 meters (some 555 feet) above the crest of a small knoll on the Mall. Constructed of white marble, the walls are 4.6 meters (15 feet) thick at the base, tapering to 45.7 centimeters (18 inches) thick at the top. The massive structure weighs 82,404.6 metric tons and rests on a foundation 11 meters (36 feet) deep.

At night floodlights illuminate the Washington Monument, and red lights at the top warn away airplanes. Only the door at the base and the paired windows on each side at the top break the Monument's smooth surface.

From these windows 152.4 meters (500 feet) above the ground visitors can enjoy a breathtaking panorama of the entire capital city, the Potomac River, the Tidal Basin, and parts of Virginia and Maryland. Visitors can ride an elevator to the chamber in the base of the cap in about 70 seconds. A stairway with 898 steps and 50 landings also ascends the shaft, but it is closed to the public.

Each July 4, Independence Day is celebrated on the Monument grounds, with festivities culminating in a gigantic fireworks display beginning at nightfall.

The Monument stands today as a familiar Washington landmark and a lasting symbol of veneration by people all over the world for one of the greatest heroes of American history.

On the Mall, Constitution Avenue at 15th Street, N.W. Facilities: Restrooms/Telephones/ Snack bar/Accessible by wheelchair

From the windows of the Washington Monument visitors can enjoy a spectacular panorama of Washington, D.C.

The bronze statue of Jefferson by Rudulph Evans portrays one of the United States' most respected founders.

THE JEFFERSON MEMORIAL

Thomas Jefferson wanted to be remembered for three accomplishments: authorship of the Declaration of Independence, authorship of the Virginia law establishing religious freedom, and the founding of the University of Virginia.

When delegates from the British colonies were debating independence from Great Britain at the Second Continental Congress, a young intellectual from Virginia, 33-year-old Thomas Jefferson, was asked to write a formal declaration of their grievances to be sent to King George III. The Congress made a few changes in his draft and on July 4, 1776, adopted the statement that set forth their reasons for severing political ties with Great Britain. Americans celebrate the anniversary of that date as Independence Day, with a festive holiday of parades, orations, and fireworks.

At the time the Declaration of Independence was written, the concept of democracy it espoused was considered radical. Yet the document has proved to be one of the most inspiring and influential documents ever written, because it eloquently outlined a new theory of government *by the people governed.* "All men are created equal," Jefferson wrote; "they are endowed by their Creator with certain inalienable rights . . . life, liberty, and the pursuit of happiness." The declaration reasoned that governments exist in order to secure these rights; that they derive their authority from the people; and that when a government tyrannizes its people, the people have the right to replace the government.

After the successful conclusion of the American Revolutionary War, Jefferson was appointed first as minister to France, then as the new country's first secretary of state. Later he was elected its second vice-president, and finally its third president.

As president from 1801 to 1809, Thomas Jefferson's vision led to the expansion of U.S. borders westward. He negotiated the purchase in 1803 of the French territory of Louisiana from Emperor Napoleon Bonaparte. This vast acquisition doubled the size of the United States, enormously increased its resources, and guaranteed that the new nation would take its place among the powers of the world.

After his presidency, Jefferson devoted himself to establishing the University of Virginia. A talented architect, Jefferson himself designed the original buildings of the university, the Virginia state capitol building in Richmond, his home Monticello, near Charlottesville, Virginia, and many other houses in Virginia. The round, colonnaded Jefferson Memorial on the shore of the Tidal Basin in Washington, D.C., echoes the classical architectural style Jefferson favored and had used at the university and in his home.

The Jefferson Memorial was dedicated in 1943 on the two hundredth anniversary of Jefferson's birth. Above the entrance, a bas-relief depicts Jefferson standing before the committee that asked him to write the Declaration of Independence.

Quotations from Jefferson's writings inscribed on the interior walls surrounding the heroic bronze statue of Jefferson set forth his basic beliefs. In the first panel, phrases from the Declaration of Independence specify his belief in the freedom of the mind. The next panel states Jefferson's beliefs in freedom from slavery and in education for ordinary people. The final inscription expresses his conviction that laws and government must change in response to changing circumstances. The quotation that encircles the chamber sums up his philosophy: "I have sworn upon the altar of God eternal hostility against every form of tyranny over the mind of man."

The beautiful Japanese cherry trees surrounding the Tidal Basin adjacent to the Jefferson Memorial were presented to the city of Washington by the city of Tokyo in 1912. Each spring they encircle the Tidal Basin in a froth of pale pink blossoms. The annual Cherry Blossom Festival is held in late March or early April.

Thousands of visitors enjoy strolling under the blossom-laden branches and photographing the Jefferson Memorial and the Monument reflected in the Tidal Basin. Indeed, the Japanese cherry trees provide a suitable setting for the national memorial to one of this nation's most brilliant, accomplished, and revered founders.

South Bank of the Tidal Basin. Facilities: Restrooms/Telephone/ Accessible by wheelchair

THE WHITE HOUSE

"Heaven bestow the best of blessings on this house, and on all that shall hereafter inhabit it. May none but honest and wise men ever rule under this roof." John Adams, second president of the United States from 1797 to 1801, wrote this prayer in 1800 the evening after he moved into the still unfinished White House for the final four months of his term of office.

Life in the White House was difficult for the Adams family. Plagued by moisture, the family burned great quantities of firewood in an attempt to dry out the damp walls. The mansion was inadequately furnished, and Mrs. Adams wrote her daughter that she used the East Room—the "great hall" designed for major state functions—to hang out the family laundry. There was no fenced yard then, where she could hang it outside.

Thomas Jefferson, third president from 1801 to 1809, began to furnish the mansion more adequately with elegant French furnishings. He enjoyed fine wines and pursued a wide range of intellectual interests, yet his informal personal style was consistent with his democratic beliefs. He began the practice of shaking hands with callers, instead of merely bowing; and he received callers of all walks of life at any reasonable hour.

The term of James Madison, fourth president from 1809 to 1817, ushered in the Golden Age of social life in the White House. President Madison's vivacious wife Dolley was the most flamboyant hostess who ever lived in the White House. She loved to entertain, and she welcomed guests of all political persuasions with equal warmth. Her charm and friendliness endeared her to all.

This era came to a sudden halt when British troops invaded the capital in 1814 and set fire to many public buildings, including the White House. Before fleeing to safety, Dolley managed to save some draperies, important papers, books, silver—and a large Gilbert Stuart portrait of George Washington. The fire left the mansion a blackened shell that had to be rebuilt and refurnished. The portrait was eventually returned to the White House. It is the only object that has been property of the White House since 1800. It now hangs in the East Room.

The East Room occupies the entire east end of the State Floor. Currently it is decorated in white and gold, with a honey-toned oak parquet floor and huge crystal chandeliers. The room is used for a variety of formal and informal occasions.

The Cross Hall connects the East Room and the State Dining Room, on the opposite side of the mansion. Three reception rooms open from this spacious hall—the Green Room, the Blue Room, and the Red Room.

The Green Room, decorated in American Sheraton style of about 1810, is used today as an informal parlor. It has a delicate green watered-silk wall covering and a crystal chandelier. It is furnished with many pieces attributed to the New York cabinetmaker Duncan Phyfe. The white marble mantel is one of a pair ordered from London after the fire of 1814.

The elegant oval Blue Room—the formal State reception room—is decorated with two-toned cream satin wall covering and blue silk upholstery and draperies. Both the oval Chinese rug and the French gilt-bronze and glass chandelier date from the nineteenth century. The furnishings reflect the French Empire period. Several of the gilded chairs are originals by Bellangé, cabinetmaker to Louis XVI, King of France.

The Red Room is used for small receptions. Furnished in Empire style, its walls and furniture are covered with sumptuous cherry-colored silk embellished with a gold wreath pattern. The chandelier is of gilded wood. The mantel matches the one in the Green Room.

The State Dining Room, in which 140 guests can be seated, repeats the white and gold color scheme of the East Room. Above the mantel hangs a portrait of Abraham Lincoln. The mantel itself is adorned with carved bison heads, and John Adams' inspirational prayer is incised into the front of the mantel.

The president's living quarters on the second floor are not open to the public.

1600 Pennsylvania Avenue, N.W. Facilities nearby on the Ellipse: Restrooms/Telephones/Accessible by wheelchair

National Park Service: Fred R. Bell

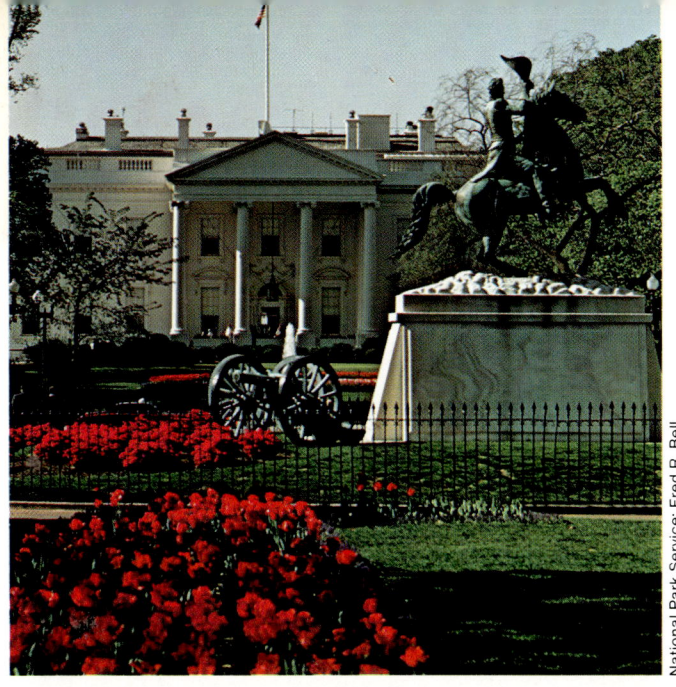

The original design of the White House was drawn up by James Hoban, an Irish-born architect. The East Room (below) has been used for a variety of occasions, including state receptions, press conferences, entertainments, weddings, and funerals. The portrait of Martha Washington was painted by Eliphalet Andrews in the late nineteenth century to hang as a companion to Gilbert Stuart's 1797 painting of George Washington that Dolley Madison saved from the fire of 1814 (inside front cover).

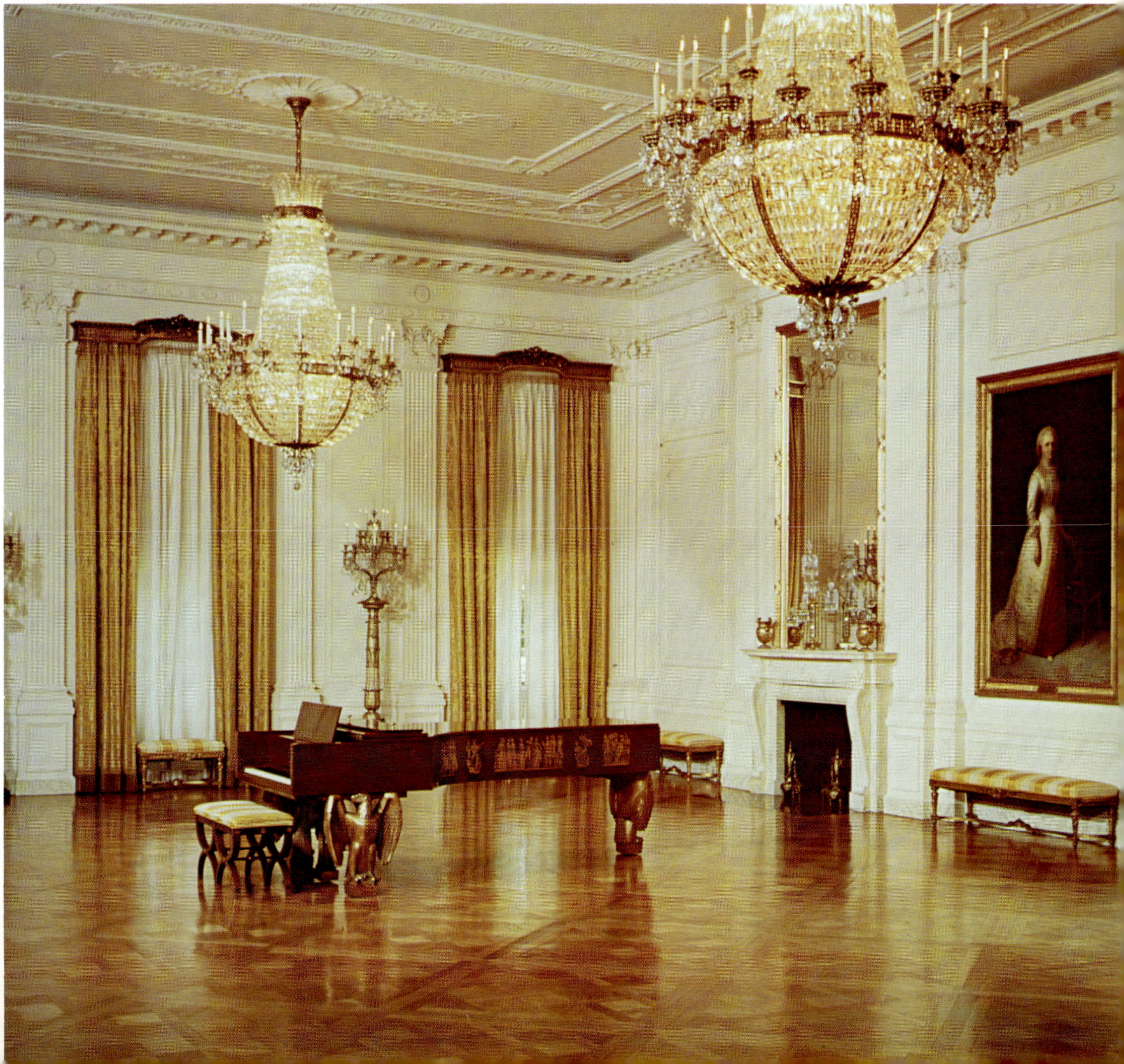

© White House Historical Association. Photograph by National Geographic Society

The design for the Capitol by Dr. William Thornton, amateur architect, was selected in a public competition, but the original design has been much altered and expanded since the Capitol was built. The bronze Statue of Freedom by sculptor Thomas Crawford was cast in five sections from the plaster original and was set in place atop the dome in 1863.

THE CAPITOL

Dominating the capital city from the crest of Capitol Hill is the "house of the people." Here the Congress—the elected representatives of the people—assemble to pass the laws that govern the nation.

President George Washington laid the cornerstone of the Capitol in 1793. But the building was still unfinished when Congress first met here in 1800, and it did not attain most of its present size and shape until 1867.

The Great Rotunda, an immense circular hall more than 29 meters (96 feet) in diameter, rises 55.8 meters (183 feet) to the inside of the central dome. A painting in the center of the dome symbolizes the national reverence for George Washington. Oil paintings hanging on the walls depict scenes from early American history, such as the landing of Columbus and the signing of the Declaration of Independence. A painted frieze encircling the hall above the paintings portrays 400 years of American history, from the landing of Columbus to the birth of aviation.

The great dome is constructed of two iron shells, one inside the other, painted white to match the marble of the rest of the building. A lantern atop the dome is lighted whenever the Congress is meeting at night. Crowning the top of the lantern is the Statue of Freedom, represented by a woman 5.8 meters (19 feet) tall. She wears a helmet adorned with stars and an American eagle.

The House of Representatives meets in the south wing; the Senate meets in the north wing. A flag flies atop each wing whenever that house is in session. Each state is represented in the Senate with two Senators and in the House of Representatives according to the population of the state. Galleries overlooking the House and Senate chambers enable visitors to observe the legislature in action. American citizens must obtain a pass from their senator or representative to gain access to the visitor's galleries while Congress is in session. Foreign visitors may obtain free temporary passes from the Doorkeeper of the House (Room H-154) and from the Senate Sergeant at Arms (Room S-321) by showing their passport or other identification.

Besides the galleries, Statuary Hall south of the Great Rotunda is perhaps the most interesting room in the Capitol. The House of Representatives met in this semicircular room from 1807 to 1857 until larger quarters were built. A brass disk in the floor marks the location of John Quincy Adams' desk when he served in Congress after his presidency (1825-1829). It was purported that, because of an acoustical peculiarity of the hall, he could listen to the whispered conferences of his political opponents on the opposite side of the room while he pretended to doze. The statues represent notable state personnages. Other statues from this collection are displayed throughout the building.

The Capitol is decorated throughout with paintings, murals, and statuary that illustrate themes of American history. One uniquely American design innovation is the tobacco and maize motifs on some column capitals. Painted capitals with tobacco motifs can be seen in the small Senate Rotunda north of the Great Rotunda. The foyer outside the Old Supreme Court Chamber on the ground floor has columns with maize motifs.

The Crypt, a circular hall on the ground floor directly under the Great Rotunda, contains exhibits detailing the history and construction of the Capitol building, as well as the tomb intended for, but never occupied by, George Washington.

In the basement, subways connect the Capitol with Senate and House office buildings so legislators can travel quickly and conveniently to their meeting chambers.

These office buildings flank both sides of the park surrounding the Capitol. Because of the location of the Capitol and its nearby office buildings on Capitol Hill, the Congress itself is referred to locally as "The Hill"—symbol of lawmaking activity and power.

The Capitol grounds are landscaped with many flowering plants and with a fine arboretum of native and exotic species of trees. Many of the trees are identified by labels on their trunks. The park provides a handsome setting for one of the nation's most cherished public buildings.

Capitol Hill. Facilities: Restrooms/ Telephones/Accessible by wheelchair

THE SUPREME COURT

"I am unaware that any nation of the globe has hitherto organized a judicial power in the same manner as the Americans," Alexis de Toqueville, French social and political observer commented in 1835. "A more imposing judicial power was never constituted by any people." Since de Toqueville wrote these words, several other countries have established judicial systems with similar power.
The power of the U.S. Supreme Court derives from its role as guardian and interpreter of the Constitution of the United States, the document that guarantees U.S. citizens their rights.

When the Founding Fathers wrote the Constitution of the United States in 1787, they organized the government into three separate but equal branches—legislative, executive, and judicial. They gave each branch certain controls over the other two so no one branch could gain absolute power. Thus the Supreme Court can strike down congressional legislation and presidential orders if they conflict with the Constitution.

The Supreme Court, therefore, considers appeals from lower courts of cases and controversies concerning constitutional rights. It also hears cases concerning international treaties and disputes between states.

Yet the Supreme Court does not have absolute power, because the other branches of government exercise some control over appointments to the court. The president appoints judges when vacancies occur, and these appointments must be confirmed by the Senate. Once confirmed, Supreme Court judges serve for life.

The Supreme Court is composed of nine judges. The Court still retains many traditions from the time it first met in 1790. The judges wear black robes while in court; but, unlike British judges, they do not wear wigs. Quill pens still are placed on counsel tables each morning that the court sits. When the judges assemble for a sitting or a conference, each judge shakes hands with every other judge as a reminder that differences of opinion do not preclude unity of purpose.

The Court convenes from October through June. The rest of the year the judges evaluate petitions for hearings, study argued and forthcoming cases, and work on their opinions.

Beginning in 1800 the Supreme Court met for 135 years in the Capitol building. It finally moved into its own building in 1935.

The Supreme Court Building faces west toward the Capitol. Seated statues on either side of the broad entrance steps symbolize, on the left, Contemplation of Justice, and, on the right, Guardian of Law.

A double row of Corinthian columns supports a sculptured pediment. The central figure represents the Goddess of Liberty holding the scales of Justice, guarded on either side by Order and Authority. Flanking them are groups symbolizing Council and Research.

Gigantic bronze doors, which are visible only when the building is closed, are decorated with bas-relief panels representing the evolution of justice. When opened, the doors slide out of sight into a recess.

A similar portico at the opposite end of the building depicts Eastern and Mediterranean lawgivers. The central figure in the sculptured eastern pediment is Moses, with the tablets of Hebraic law. Flanking him are Confucius, the great lawgiver of China, and Solon, codifier of Greek law.

The majestic, dignified Court Chamber is embellished with Ionic colonnades, bronze grillwork, deep red velvet draperies, and sculptured marble panels. Near the side entrances to the courtroom two magnificent marble and bronze spiral staircases ascend five stories. They are supported only by attachment to the walls and by overlapping steps.

The remainder of the building is devoted to offices, conference rooms, and a library.

With its elaborate white marble Corinthian columns, monumental entrance steps, and sculptured pediments, the Supreme Court Building resembles an ancient Roman temple. And so it is a temple—a temple devoted to the mandate inscribed at its entrance: "Equal Justice Under Law."

First Street and Maryland Avenue, N.E. Facilities: Restrooms/Telephones/Cafeteria/Accessible by wheelchair

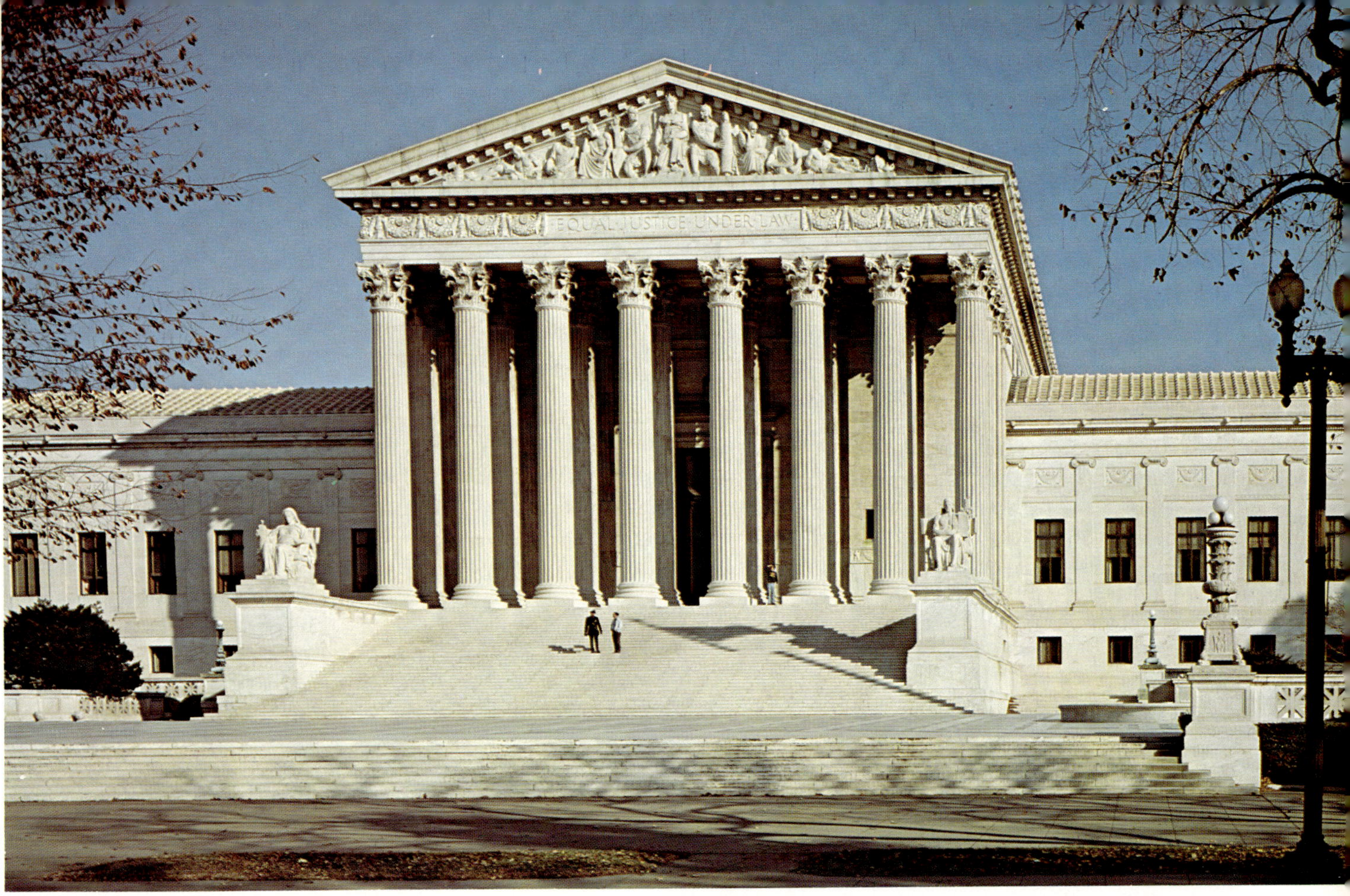

Ed Cooper

Photos © Foundation of the Federal Bar Association, by National Geogrpahic Society

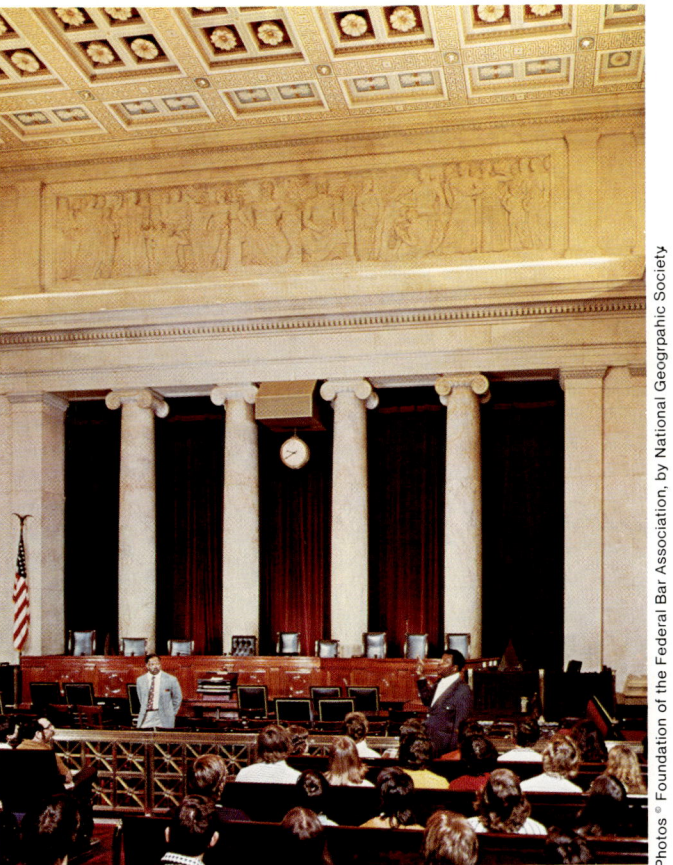

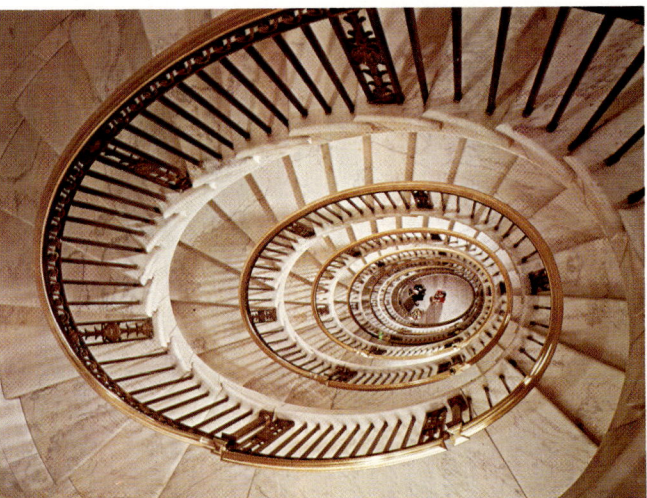

The Supreme Court Building on Capitol Hill was completed in 1935. The dignified courtroom of the highest tribunal in the land inspires a sense of great awe. Two self-supporting cantilevered spiral staircases ascend five stories. The Paris Opera and the Vatican are among the few other places in the world with similar staircases.

ORIENTATION

The great common known as "The Mall" sweeps 2.4 kilometers (1.5 miles) westward from the Capitol as far as the Potomac River. Most of the city's major sightseeing attractions are concentrated around the Capitol and along The Mall, where they are convenient to visit on foot or by Tourmobile.

The major attractions are arranged roughly in the shape of a cross. Imagine the Capitol at the foot of the cross, the Lincoln Memorial at the head, the White House and the Jefferson Memorial at the ends of the cross arms, and the Washington Monument at the intersection. Many museums and art galleries are located along the sides.

The Capitol was planned to be the center of the City of Washington. North Capitol Street, East Capitol Street, South Capitol Street, and The Mall extend from the Capitol and divide the city into four sections—Northwest, Northeast, Southeast, and Southwest. Most tourist attractions are in the Northwest section.

Streets were laid out in a grid pattern. Numbered streets run north/south in each section. Streets running east/west are lettered in alphabetical order in each section. (There are no J, X, Y, Z Streets.) At the end of the first alphabet, streets carry two-syllable names in alphabetical order. Streets in the third alphabet carry three-syllable names. The fourth alphabet has streets named after flowers and trees in alphabetical order. Avenues with state names run diagonally.

To find an address in Washington, imagine yourself standing with your back to one of the axes of the Capitol. Street addresses with odd numbers will be to your right; even numbers, to your left. Addresses increase by even hundreds with each block (A, 100; B, 200, . . . skip J . . . K, 1000 . . .).

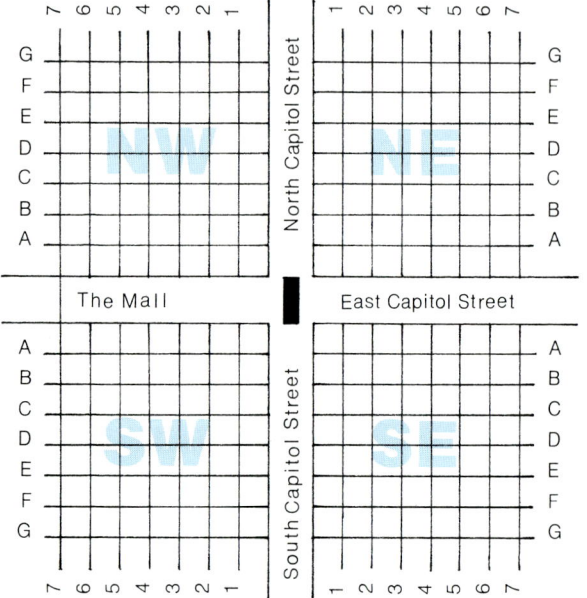

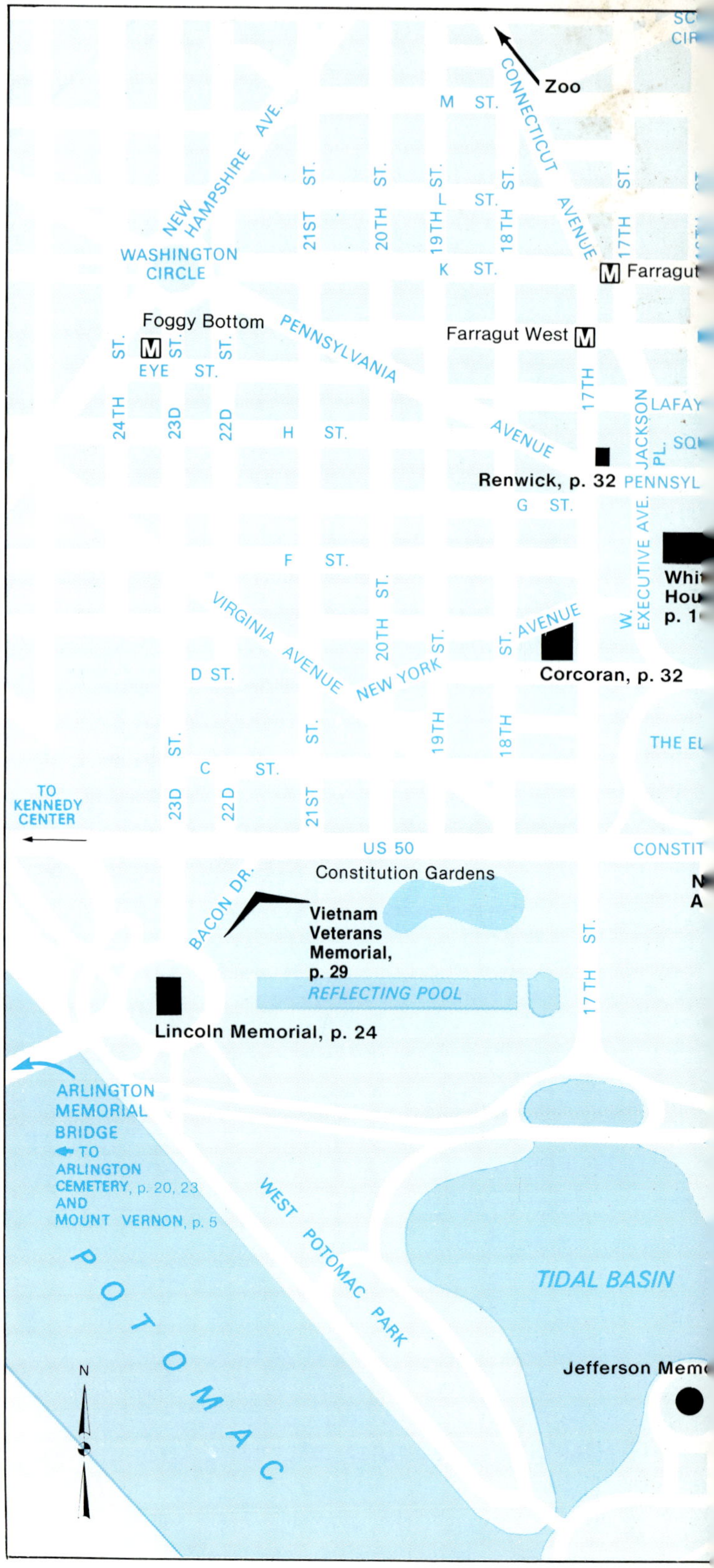

16

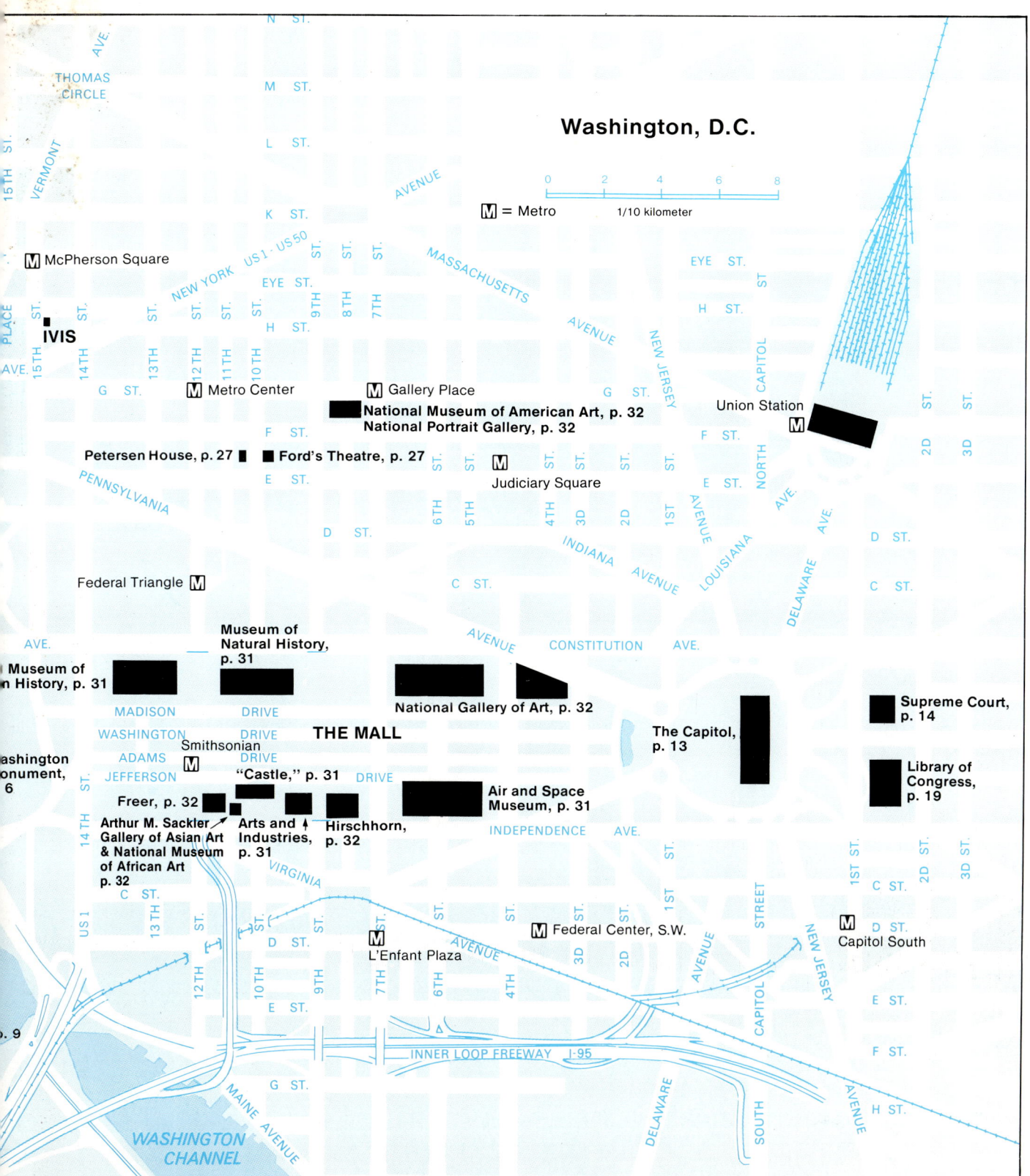

The exhibition halls of the Library of Congress display treasured items of U.S. history and early printing.

THE LIBRARY OF CONGRESS

When the government moved to Washington, D.C., in 1800, Congress authorized creation of a library to serve its reference needs. Books were ordered from England and were housed in the Capitol Building. When the British burned the Capitol in 1814, however, the library was destroyed.

The following year Congress purchased Thomas Jefferson's personal library of nearly 6,500 books to form the nucleus of a new collection. By the 1870s the library was overflowing its quarters, so Congress decided to construct a separate library building.

The Library of Congress Building, designed in the style of the Italian Renaissance, was completed in 1897. The three-story gray sandstone structure has a ribbed copper dome capped by a lantern and a torch that symbolizes the Flame of Knowledge.

At street level in front of the building a delightful fountain depicts Neptune's Court. Neptune is surrounded by nymphs riding seahorses, tritons blowing conch shell horns, and bronze frogs and sea turtles spouting water.

Panels on the three bronze entrance doors represent, from left to right, Tradition, The Art of Painting, and Writing. Sculptured busts of great men of letters are framed by circular windows above the entrance. Sculptured heads above arched windows on the first floor represent major ethnic groups of mankind.

The Great Hall just inside the entrance is lavishly ornamented with murals, sculpture, mosaic tile, stained glass, plaques, columns, arches, and arcades. The floor is laid in many colors of marble; inlaid brass signs of the zodiac border an inlaid brass compass in the center of the hall. The ceiling is decorated with printers' and publishers' marks.

The arcade opposite the entrance contains an exhibit of the *Gutenberg Bible* and *The Giant Bible of Mainz*. The latter is an outstanding example of a medieval hand-lettered, illuminated manuscript book. The *Gutenberg Bible,* produced in the same city at about the same time (1450-1455), is the first book in the Western world printed with movable type. This invention marked a milestone in the liberation of the human mind, because it enabled the publication of many copies of printed materials at once, thus widening the dissemination of knowledge.

Six painted panels in this room trace the evolution of communication. First, prehistoric man piles up stones as a marker; then an Oriental storyteller tells a tale in the oral tradition; Egyptians chisel hieroglyphics on a tomb; an American Indian draws a pictograph on a buffalo skin; a monk hand-letters a manuscript book; and Gutenberg prints a book on his printing press.

The balustrade of the white Italian marble stairway leading to the second floor is sculpted with lively cherubs holding objects that symbolize various arts and sciences. Cherubs atop the stair piers represent the continents.

From the second floor one has a good view of the heroic mosaic mural of Minerva, goddess of wisdom, on an upper stair landing.

The stairs past Minerva lead to the gallery overlooking the Main Reading Room in the Rotunda. Mahogany reading desks and card catalogs surround the circular distribution counter in the center of the room. Red marble columns support giant arches on which the dome rests. A mural between the dome and the lantern symbolizes the nations and the epochs that have contributed to the progress of civilization.

Since the Library of Congress was built, annexes have had to be constructed to accommodate the expanding collections of books, periodicals, manuscripts, maps, musical scores, photographs, prints, drawings, motion picture reels, phonograph records, tapes, and microfilm. The collections contain tens of millions of items, and they are growing at the rate of more than 7,000 items every working day. These extensive resources are now available not only to Congress, but also to other branches of government, to libraries, and to scholars and the general public.

10 First Street, N.E. Facilities: Restrooms/Telephones/Cafeteria/ Accessible by wheelchair

ARLINGTON HOUSE

George Washington Parke Custis is the link between two American heroes of different eras—George Washington, Revolutionary war hero and first president, and Robert E. Lee, Civil War hero.

Custis was Martha Washington's grandson whom George Washington reared as his foster son when the boy's father, John Parke Custis, died. After George and Martha Washington died, Custis started building his home on a 445-hectare (1,100-acre) estate in Virginia he had inherited from his father. Two years later, in 1804, Custis was married, and the couple set up housekeeping in the partially completed house. Arlington, as Custis named the house, was finally finished in 1817.

Custis and his wife had only one surviving child, Mary Anna Randolph. She married a handsome young graduate of the West Point military academy, Robert E. Lee, whom she had known since childhood, and the young couple moved into Arlington House with her parents.

Lee was away from home on military duty much of the 30 years he and Mary called Arlington their home, but he loved the estate more than any other place in the world.

In early 1861 civil strife was imminent. At President Lincoln's request, Lee was summoned to Washington and was offered the command of the U.S. Army. The Army would invade Virginia if war broke out. When Lee learned that Virginia had seceded from the Union, he was deeply distressed. He was torn between family ties in his native state dating back six generations, and loyalty to the Union, which he had served as an Army officer for 30 years. He secluded himself in his bedroom on the night of April 19, 1861, while family and friends waited anxiously below for his decision. Lee decided to resign his commission in the U.S. Army. Two days later he rode away in civilian clothes to offer his services to the state of Virginia. He never returned to Arlington. His wife and family left shortly thereafter.

As the leader of the Confederate Army, General Robert E. Lee's noble character and military genius made him the hero of the South and the respected adversary of the North. After the Confederacy was defeated in 1865, Lee served as president of Washington College in Lexington, Virginia, until his death in 1870. The college was renamed Washington and Lee University in his honor.

Arlington House has been restored to its approximate appearance just before the Civil War. The house is constructed of bricks formed of native clay overlaid by stucco. The exterior is painted to resemble marble. The colonnaded portico of eight huge Doric columns supports a massive classical pediment.

The large scale of the exterior is preserved inside the house. With its high ceiling, tall doors, and cross-ventilation, the center hall was used as a summer parlor. High on the walls are still visible animal scenes that Custis, an artist, painted on wet plaster when the house was new. North of the center hall are the family parlor, where Robert E. Lee and Mary Randolph Custis were married, and the family dining room, where before breakfast on summer mornings Lee used to place a rosebud beside the plate of each of his daughters.

Upstairs, to the right, is the bedroom where General Lee had agonized over his fateful choice.

Although some of the furnishings in the mansion are originals, many furnishings had been lost in the war, dispersed to heirs, or sent to Mount Vernon or the National Museum. Where originals are not available, replicas of original pieces or furnishings of the period are being used in the restoration.

From its impressive location atop a hill on the Virginia shore of the Potomac River, Arlington House commands a panorama that the Marquis de Lafayette described as the "finest view in the world"— and is itself visible from much of Washington, D.C., especially at night when it is floodlighted.

Arlington House not only is a fine example of antebellum architecture in the United States. It is an enduring memorial to Robert E. Lee, Confederate hero honored by both North and South and the personification of the agony of civil war that rent the Union.

In Arlington National Cemetery, Arlington, Virginia, via Memorial Bridge. Facilities: Restrooms/ Telephone/Accessible by wheelchair with assistance

Eugenia Horstman

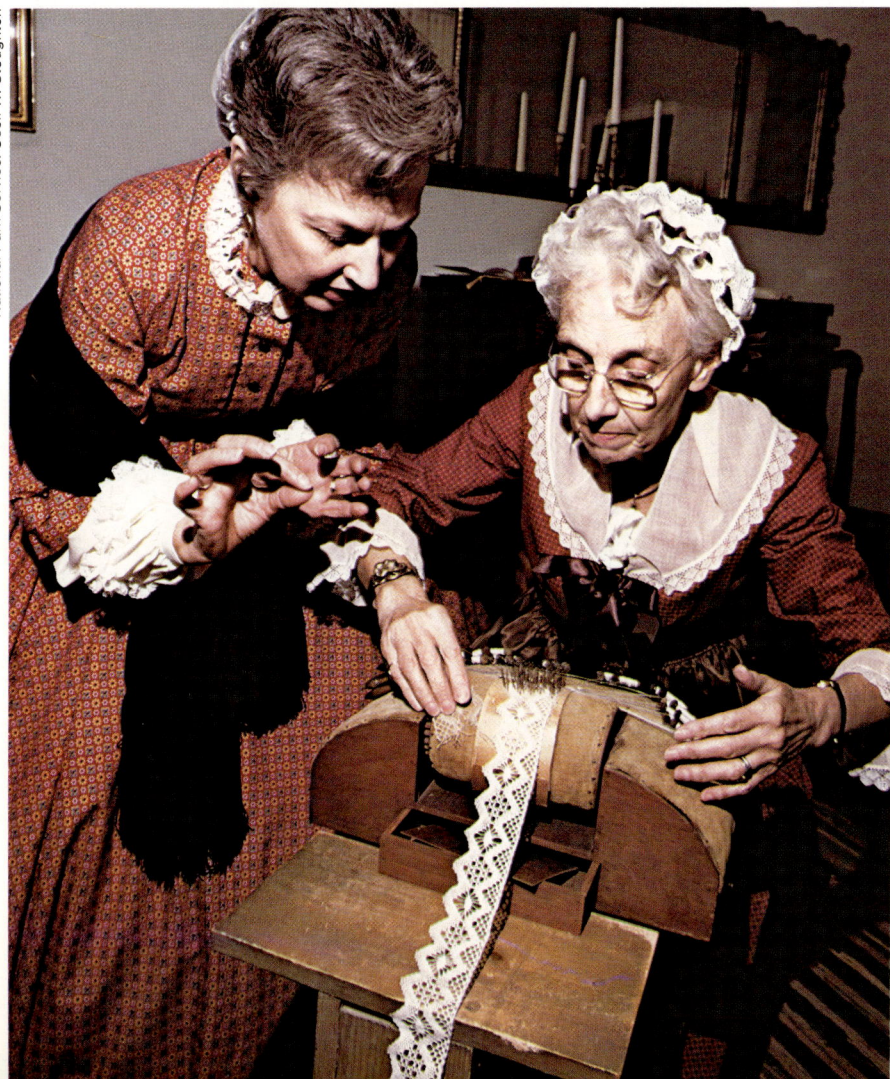

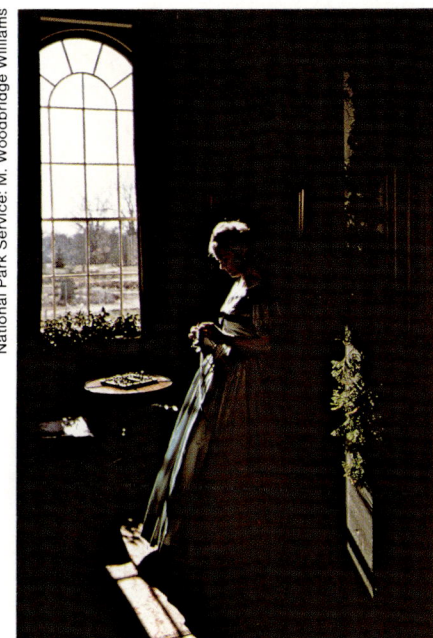

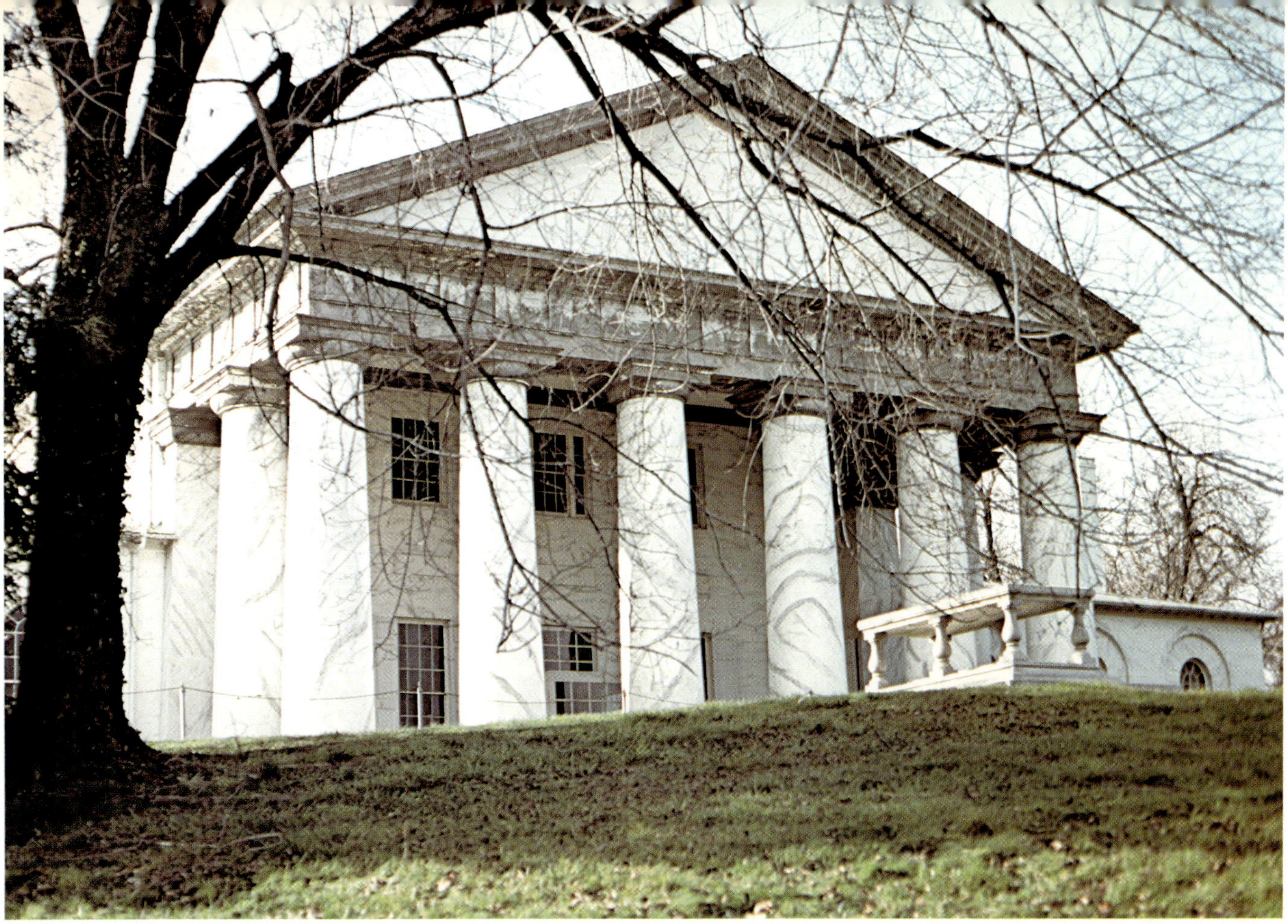

National Park Service: Cecil W. Stoughton

National Park Service: M. Woodbridge Williams

The home of Confederate General Robert E. Lee is being restored to its antebellum appearance. Women in period costume help demonstrate the way of life of that era. The tablelike marker in front of the mansion marks the grave of Pierre L'Enfant, original designer of Washington, D.C.

Eugenia Horstman

National Park Service: Fred Bell

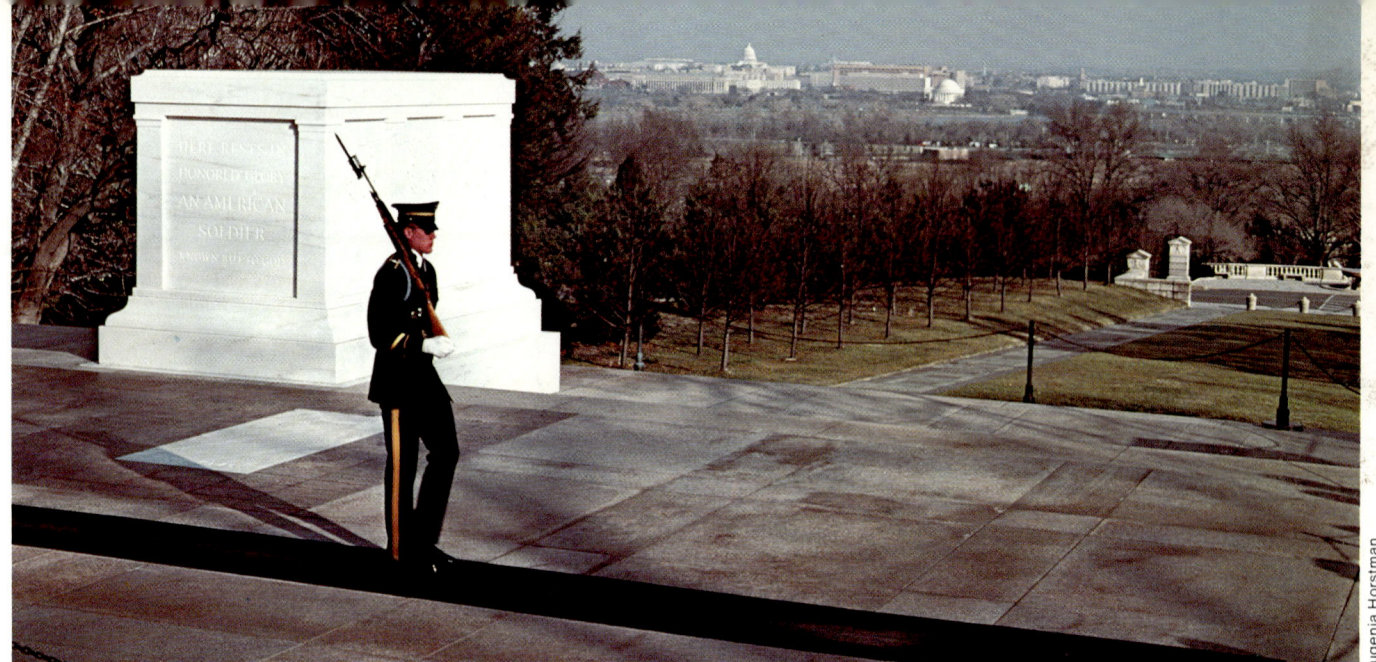

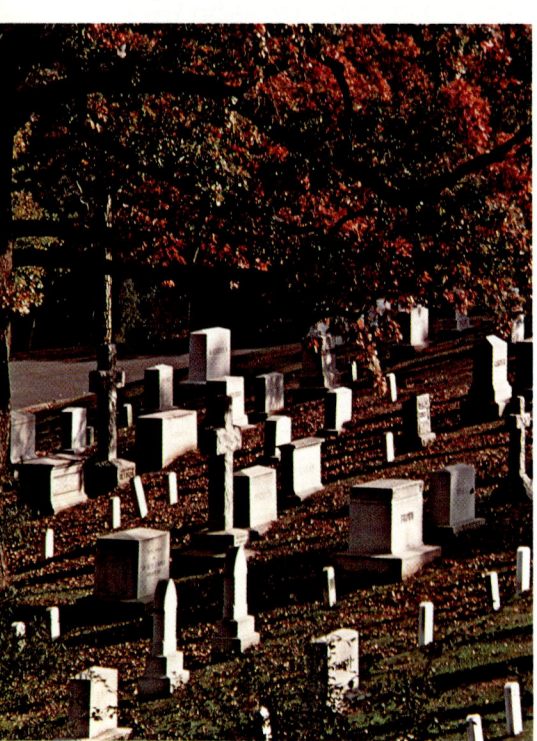

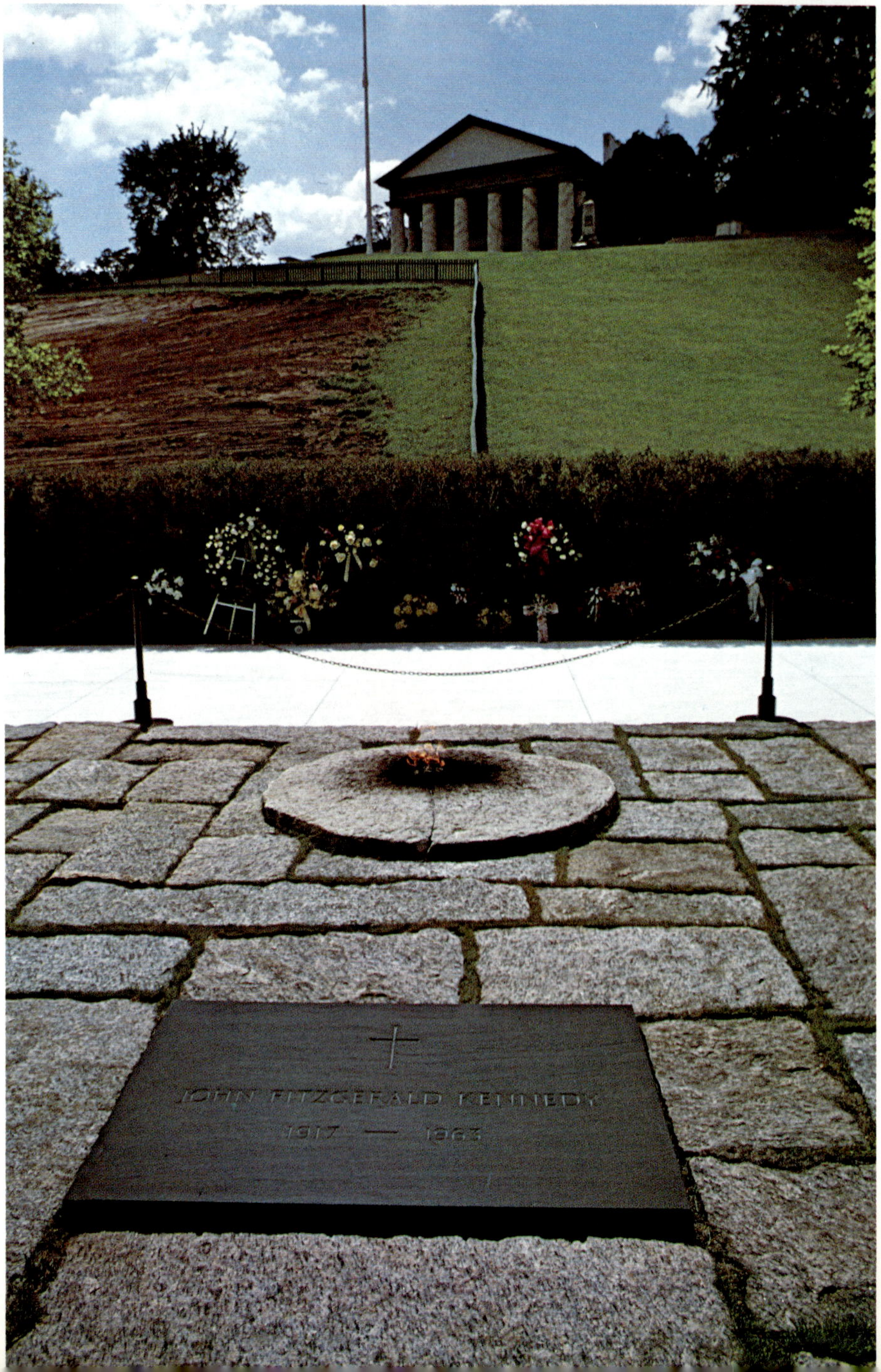

National Park Service: Cecil W. Stoughton

A lone sentinel maintains vigil night and day at the Tomb of the Unknown Soldier. Arlington National Cemetery contains graves of military personnel from all wars the United States has fought. Many famous people are buried here as well. On the hillside below Arlington House an eternal flame marks the grave of President John Fitzgerald Kennedy. His brother Robert Kennedy is buried nearby.

ARLINGTON NATIONAL CEMETERY

A month after Robert E. Lee rode away from Arlington House to join the Confederacy, Union forces occupied his estate. His home became Union headquarters for the defense of the city of Washington during most of the Civil War.

When Mrs. Lee could not personally appear in the midst of the war in 1864 to pay property taxes, the federal government confiscated the property. The mansion and 80 hectares (200 acres) of ground surrounding the house were designated a military cemetery.

After Robert E. Lee died in 1870, one of his sons claimed that the estate had been illegally confiscated and that he was the rightful owner under the will of his grandfather, George Washington Parke Custis. After more than a decade of litigation, the case was finally settled when the Supreme Court decided against the government in favor of Lee. By that time, though, thousands of graves surrounded the house, so Lee sold the property to the federal government.

Interment in Arlington National Cemetery is reserved mainly for selected military personnel, their spouses, and dependent children. Officers and enlisted men from all wars the United States has fought are buried here. In addition, many famous people—civilian as well as military—are buried at Arlington; for example, George Washington Parke Custis and Mary Custis, builders of Arlington House; Admiral Robert E. Peary, discoverer of the North Pole; William Howard Taft, president from 1909 to 1913; John J. Pershing, General of the Armies in World War I; and General George Marshall of World War II fame.

Partway down the hill in front of Arlington House an eternal flame marks the grave of President John Fitzgerald Kennedy. An infant son and daughter who had died before he was killed lie on either side of their father. A few steps down from the grave site an elliptical plaza is bordered on one side by a low wall on which are engraved excerpts from Kennedy's inaugural address in 1961. Among them is his most famous quotation:

"And so my fellow Americans, ask not what your country can do for you. Ask what you can do for your country. My fellow citizens of the world, ask not what America will do for you, but what together we can do for the freedom of man."

Nearby, at the end of a short walkway, is the grave of President Kennedy's younger brother, Robert Kennedy.

The white marble Memorial Amphitheater on a hilltop near Arlington House was completed in 1920. It was built to accommodate services commemorating military dead held here each Memorial Day, May 30.

On the paved plaza east of the Amphitheater rests a massive but simple sarcophagus of white marble. This is the Tomb of the Unknown Soldier. Beneath the Tomb lies an unidentified soldier killed in Europe in World War I. The front panel of the Tomb depicts three figures symbolizing Victory through Valor attaining Peace. On the rear panel is inscribed the words, "Here rests in honored glory an American Soldier known but to God." On the plaza west of the Tomb marble slabs mark crypts of unknown soldiers from World War II and the Korean conflict.

A lone sentinel guards the Tomb night and day, always following a precise, symbolic ritual. The ritual is based on the number 21, which represents the highest salute given dignitaries in military and state ceremonies. The sentinel paces the walkway in exactly 21 steps. He faces the Tomb for 21 seconds, turns, pauses for another 21 seconds, and retraces his steps—always bearing his weapon away from the Tomb.

The guard may not speak or alter his routine except under exceptional circumstances; for example, he will issue a warning if anyone tries to enter the restricted area around the Tomb. The impressive ceremonial changing of the guard takes place every half hour 1 April to 30 September; it occurs hourly 1 October to 31 March.

These sentinels are members of The Old Guard, the Army honor guard and escort for the president. To be selected as a Tomb guard, a man must possess exemplary qualities and be highly recommended by his superior officers.

Arlington, Virginia, via Memorial Bridge. Facilities: Restrooms/ Telephone/Accessible by wheelchair

THE LINCOLN MEMORIAL

Born in a log cabin in the Kentucky backcountry, Abraham Lincoln did not have the advantages of wealth, social position, or good schooling. But he had intelligence and determination. As a youth Lincoln labored long over his books by firelight and kerosene lamp, and he later became proficient in the law.

After he made a name for himself as a lawyer, Lincoln was elected first to the Illinois state legislature, then to the U.S. Congress, then to the presidency. He brought to public office warmth, honesty, wit, logic, and political shrewdness. But six weeks after he was inaugurated in 1861, the Civil War erupted over the issues of states rights and slavery. President Lincoln faced the most difficult task any American president has ever faced—reuniting a country divided against itself.

Lincoln believed that slavery is morally wrong, but his major aim was to restore the Union. He hesitated to liberate the slaves for fear of alienating the border states still within the Union. Therefore, in 1863 he issued an Emancipation Proclamation that freed slaves only in areas then fighting against the Union. All slaves were finally freed by Congressional amendment to the Constitution after the end of the war.

On April 9, 1865, Confederate General Robert E. Lee surrendered to Union General Ulysses S. Grant, and the Civil War was over. Five days later an assassin's bullet felled President Lincoln.

Construction of the Lincoln Memorial began in 1914, and work was finished in 1921. A site was selected on a line with the Washington Monument and the Capitol. The site was on marsh land in the Potomac River that had been filled in, so great care had to be taken that the building would not sink into the unstable soil. Consequently, the Lincoln Memorial was constructed on great concrete pillars that extend 13 to 19.8 meters (44 to 65 feet) to bedrock. Then soil was built up around the foundation so that the building seems to be resting on a small hill. An exhibit in a chamber under the memorial to the left of the entrance steps illustrates details of construction.

The beautiful memorial of classical Greek design faces east toward the Mall. The 36 fluted Doric columns in the outer colonnade represent the states in the Union at the time of Lincoln's death. Their names are inscribed on the frieze above the columns. The names of the 48 states in the Union when the building was completed are inscribed on the attic wall above the frieze.

The seated statue of Lincoln is 5.8 meters high and 5.8 meters wide (19 feet by 19 feet). At that scale, the figure would be 8.5 meters (28 feet) tall if it were standing. Behind the statue is inscribed the dedication, "In this temple as in the hearts of the people for whom he saved the Union the memory of Abraham Lincoln is enshrined forever."

The memorial chamber also contains eight Ionic columns and two huge stone tablets inscribed with quotations from Lincoln that epitomize his ideals. Lincoln's famous Gettysburg Address is inscribed on the south wall. This short but eloquent speech was made at the consecration of the burial ground at Gettysburg, Pennsylvania, where tens of thousands of countrymen had died fighting each other in just one battle of the Civil War. The speech called for reunification of the divided country "that this nation, under God, shall have a new birth of freedom; and that government of the people, by the people, for the people, shall not perish from the earth." Above this statement a mural depicts an Angel of Truth freeing a slave. Groups of figures on either side symbolize Justice and Immortality.

Lincoln's Second Inaugural Address, which emphasizes his compassion and hope for healing, is inscribed on the north wall. The mural above it symbolizes Reunion of the North and South. Groups of figures on the left and right symbolize Fraternity and Charity.

It seems not at all incongruous that Abraham Lincoln, the man born in a log cabin, should be commemorated by a classical Greek temple. The example of his thought, character, and deeds has won for him a place in the American "pantheon" forever.

On the Mall at 23d Street, N.W. Facilities: Restrooms/Telephone/ Accessible by wheelchair

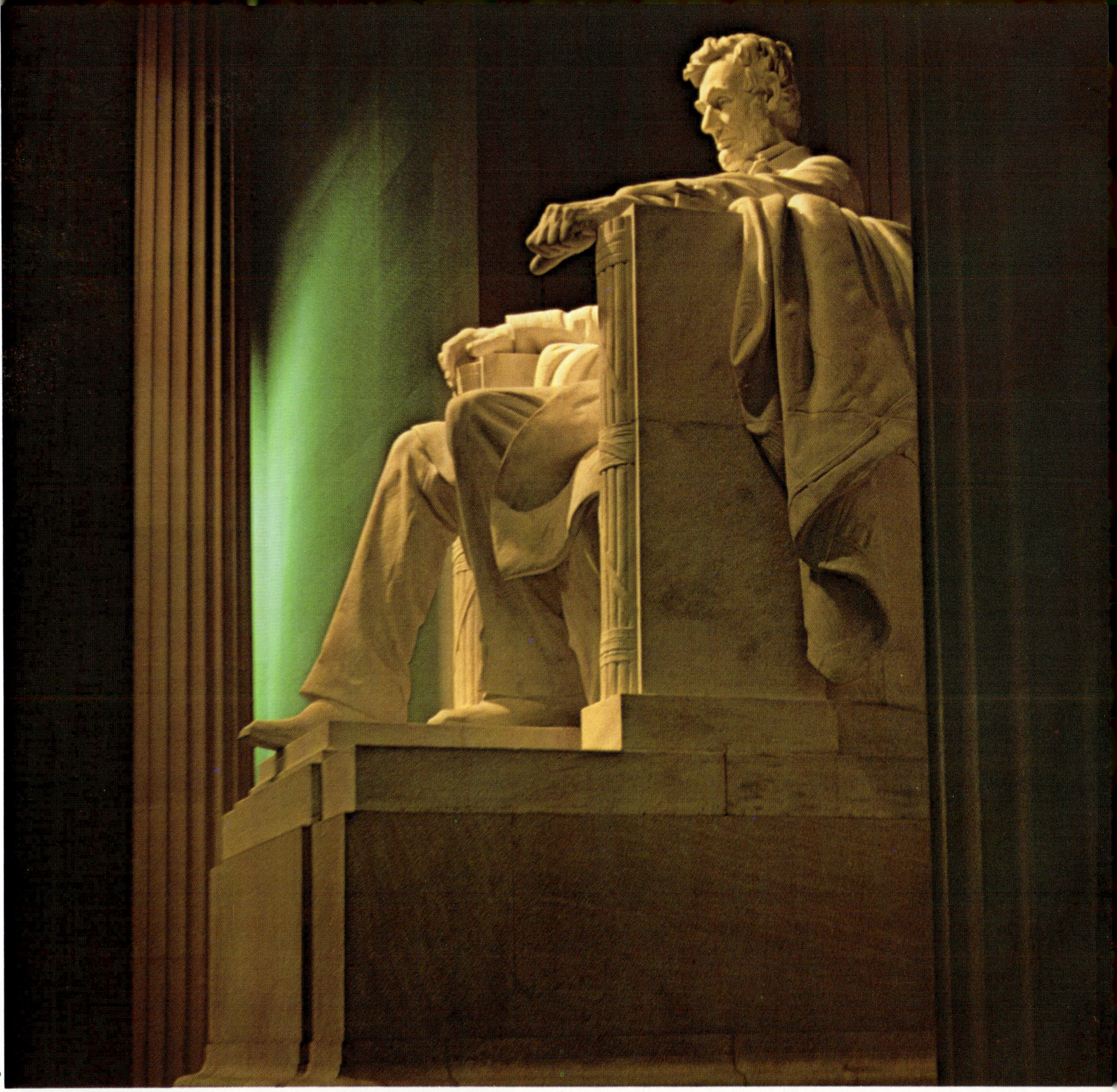

Eugenia Horstman

National Park Service: Cecil W. Stoughton

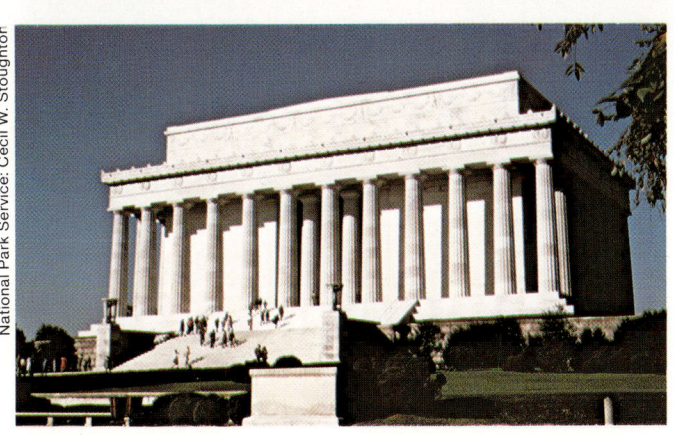

Henry Bacon designed the simple, classic Lincoln Memorial, which was dedicated in 1922. Daniel Chester French designed the statue of Abraham Lincoln. The statue was cut from 20 blocks of marble, which are so perfectly interlocked that the statue seems to be formed from one huge block.

Ford's Theatre, where President Abraham Lincoln was shot on 14 April 1865, and the Petersen House across the street, where he died, have been restored to their appearance on that tragic day. A museum in the basement of the theater depicts various phases of Lincoln's life. The theater again presents theatrical performances after having been closed after the assassination.

Ford's Theater, Eugenia Horstman

Petersen House, National Park Service

National Park Service: M. Woodbridge Williams

FORD'S THEATRE

Early in April 1865 President Abraham Lincoln had an ominous premonition. He dreamed he was awakened by the sound of sobbing. He arose and followed the sound to the East Room, where a shrouded figure lay in state surrounded by mourners. One of the honor guards on duty whispered, "The President—killed by an assassin."

Within two weeks Lincoln lay in state in the East Room of the White House surrounded by mourners.

On April 14, 1865, President and Mrs. Lincoln attended a play at Ford's Theatre with Major Henry R. Rathbone and his fiancee. They sat in a flag-draped box that rested on the apron of the stage.

During the second scene of the third act, when the audience burst into laughter at an actor's line, a woman suddenly screamed. A man leaped from the president's box onto the stage, stumbled, and hobbled off-stage shouting, "Sic semper tyrannis!" (Thus always tyrants!) Lincoln lay mortally wounded with a bullet hole behind his left ear.

Doctors in the audience rushed to the president's side. They advised against the rough trip over cobblestone streets back to the White House, so Lincoln was carried across the street to the boarding house of William Petersen.

While Lincoln lay dying in a back bedroom, Mrs. Lincoln kept vigil in the front parlor and Secretary of War Stanton interviewed witnesses. Lincoln died at 7:22 the following morning without regaining consciousness.

John Wilkes Booth, a prominent actor who was bitterly disappointed at the outcome of the Civil War, was the assassin. He had quietly entered the president's box and barred the door behind him to prevent anyone from following him. Booth knew the play well. He waited for the moment when only one actor was onstage and laughter would muffle the pistol shot. After shooting Lincoln, he grappled briefly with Major Rathbone and jumped the 3.7 meters (12 feet) down onto the stage. As he jumped, his spur caught in the Treasury Guard flag decorating the box, and his awkward landing broke his leg. Nevertheless, he managed to make his way to a horse awaiting him in the alley and escaped.

Booth stopped at a physician's house several miles south of the city and had his leg tended. Twelve days later cavalry troops found him hiding in a barn in Virginia. They shot him when he refused to surrender without fighting.

Lincoln's assassination plunged the nation into grief. After lying in state, his body was placed on a funeral train that slowly made its way to his home in Springfield, Illinois, where he was buried. According to Carl Sandburg, poet and Lincoln biographer, the funeral train "took long to pass its many given points. Many millions of people saw it and personally moved in it and were part of its procession. The line of march ran seventeen hundred miles. As a death march nothing like it had ever been attempted before."

The War Department closed the theater after the assassination and stationed guards outside it. The owner planned to reopen the theater in June, but the public threatened to burn it down if he did. Therefore, the government purchased the theater and remodeled it for use as offices and storage. Later the building was used to display a collection of Lincoln memorabilia. In 1964 the building was closed for restoration to its appearance on that tragic spring night. It reopened again in 1968. The Petersen house is furnished in a manner similar to its appearance the morning the president died there.

The Lincoln Museum is now housed in the basement of the theater. It contains exhibits related to Lincoln's early life, presidential years, family life, and assassination.

Once again Ford's Theatre presents theatrical performances—but the president's box remains empty.

511 10th Street, N.W. Facilities: Restrooms/Telephone/Partially accessible by wheelchair with assistance

THE KENNEDY CENTER

As a grieving nation sought a suitable memorial to President John F. Kennedy—assassinated on November 22, 1963—it was decided to dedicate a national cultural center to his memory. Congress authorized $15.5 million for construction, and individuals and groups from all over the country contributed more than $2 million. Many nations, too, donated funds and furnishing in Kennedy's honor. For example, Italy donated all the marble for the building; Great Britain sent a sculpture by Dame Barbara Hepworth; and Australia donated seven tapestries representing The Creation, designed by John Coburn. The John F. Kennedy Center for the Performing Arts opened to the public in September 1971.

The ground floor of the massive building is divided primarily into three elegant theaters. The Eisenhower Theater is designed for dramatic productions. Canada donated the red and black stage curtain. The Opera House presents musical theater and ballet as well as opera. Japan donated the red and gold silk stage curtain; Austria gave the starburst crystal chandelier. France donated two tapestries based on Henri Matisse "cutout" designs and two sculptures by Henri Laurens for the box tier lobby. Ireland sent a Waterford crystal chandelier with four matching sconces for the South Lounge. The Concert Hall is designed for instrumental and choral performances. The crystal chandeliers are a gift from Norway. Mrs. Jouett Shouse, an American patron of the arts, donated the spectacular organ. Israel sent artworks and complete furnishings for the Lounge.

These three theaters are separated by two great halls. In the Hall of States the flags of U.S. states and territories hang in the sequence in which they entered the Union. In the Hall of Nations the flags of countries that the United States recognizes diplomatically are displayed in alphabetical order. Both great halls open onto the Grand Foyer, the immense lobby that serves all three theaters. Crystal chandeliers from Sweden and huge mirrors from Belgium brighten the 630-foot-long room. A massive bronze bust of President Kennedy dominates the foyer. A cinema also located on the ground floor shows classic motion pictures daily.

An elevator in the Hall of Nations provides access to the Roof Terrace, where the Terrace Theatre—a gift of the Japanese government—caters to very small audiences for poetry readings, small dramas by new playwrights, and experimental theater. Three rooftop restaurants cater to a variety of tastes and budgets. The outdoor terrace provides excellent views of the Potomac River, Arlington Memorial Bridge, and Georgetown.

The Kennedy Center is the product of the dreams, efforts, and gifts of many individuals and many nations. When the powerful and the humble mingle in the glittering Grand Foyer, then is the living tribute to the memory of President John F. Kennedy most vivid and most meaningful.

New Hampshire Avenue at F. Street, N.W. Facilities: Restrooms/ Telephones/Restaurants/Parking/ Accessible by wheelchair

Nations from all over the world helped build and furnish the Kennedy Center.

VIETNAM VETERANS MEMORIAL

Walk along the Wall, and you cannot avoid contemplating the tragedy of war. The Vietnam Veterans Memorial was established on the Mall to acknowledge the sacrifices of the American men and women who served in the Vietnam War (1959-1975). A black granite wall 494 feet long in the shape of a shallow recumbent V gradually slopes from ground level to 10 feet deep at its vertex, forming a vale of sorrow within its arms. The wall is inscribed with names of more than 58,000 dead or missing Americans (average age 19 years) in the chronological order of their loss. Walk past these thousands upon thousands of names, and your sense of the immense sacrifice of a generation grows increasingly painful. The sheer number of losses—tangible on this wall—is staggering.

After the war a small group of veterans founded the Vietnam Veterans Memorial Fund to raise money for a national memorial. More than $9 million raised by contributions from half a million American people, businesses, and other organizations enabled this project to be built without government money. The memorial was designed by a 21-year-old architecture student, Maya Ying Lin, who won a national design competition from among 1,421 entries.

The Vietnam Veterans Memorial was dedicated on November 13, 1982. Two years later a flagstaff and a bronze statue of three young soldiers sculpted by Frederick E. Hart were added to the entrance plaza of the memorial. The figures represent different ethnic groups that fought side-by-side in Vietnam.

Grieving visitors come to look for the name of a lost comrade or a loved one, and they sometimes leave behind tokens of remembrance tucked between the stone panels or leaning against the base of the wall—flowers, a letter or snapshot, a childhood toy, a battle medal. The polished surface of the wall reflects the images of mourners upon the roster of names, symbolically uniting them in life and death.

Constitution Avenue at 21st Street, N.W. Accessible by wheelchair

© 1987 Lara Kay Connally

Among the popular exhibits in the museums along The Mall are the Hope Diamond, the Insect Zoo, the Wright Flyer, and the First Ladies Hall. The Red Room display (below) depicts the gowns of (from left to right) Mrs. Carter, Mrs. Ford, Mrs. Nixon, Mrs. Johnson, and Mrs. Kennedy.

Smithsonian Institution

Smithsonian Institution

Smithsonian Institution

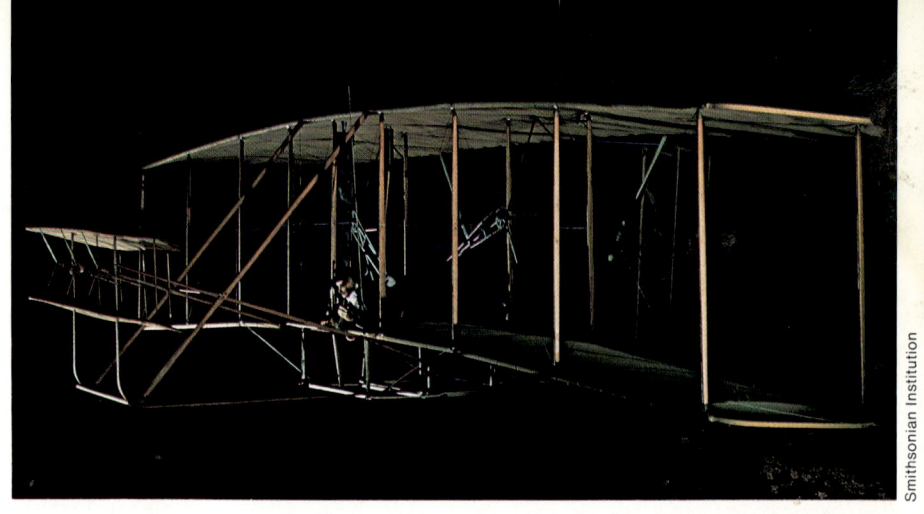

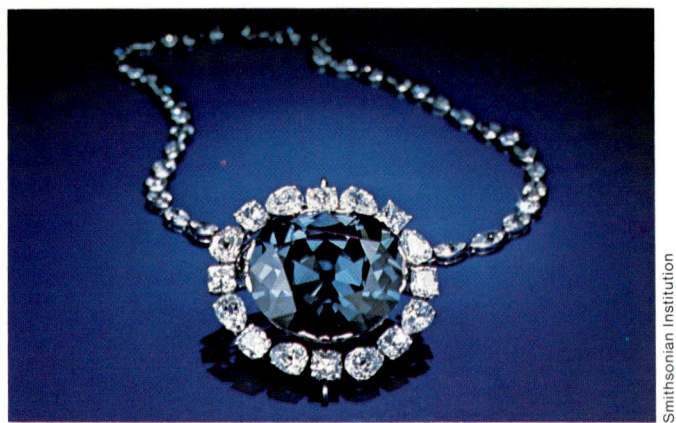

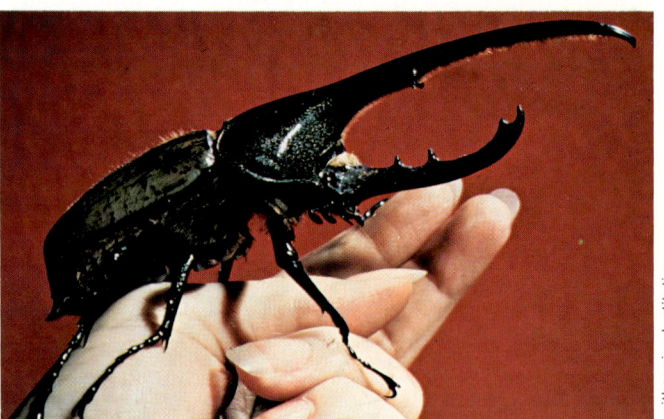

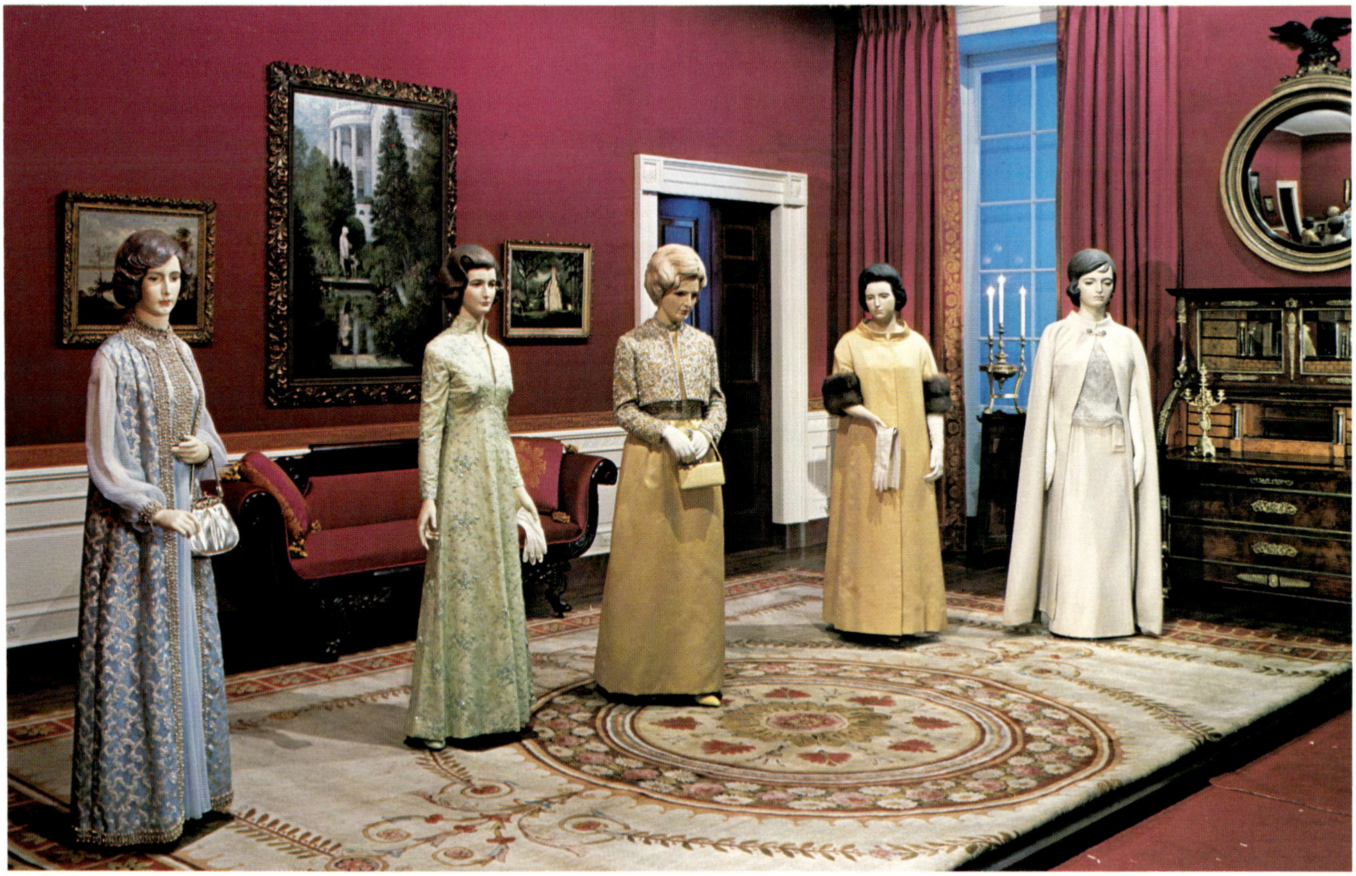

Smithsonian Institution

THE MUSEUMS

Although basic research is the primary purpose of the Smithsonian Institution and 99 percent of its objects are retained for study in research collections, the objects on public display cover an astounding range of scientific disciplines and human endeavor.

No dusty archive, the Smithsonian Institution takes great care to create lively, authentic exhibits—even to the point of accompanying them, in some cases, with realistic sounds and aromas. Special exhibits, demonstrations, lectures, classes, concerts, festivals, and even kite-flying contests contribute to the cultural life of the city.

The fanciful structure known as the Castle was completed in 1855. It contains a visitor's information center, administrative offices, and the crypt of the Englishman James Smithson, who bequeathed half a million dollars to the United States in 1835 to establish the Smithsonian Institution.

The red brick Arts and Industries Building next to the Castle contains the finest objects of Victorian Americana exhibited at the Philadelphia Centennial Exposition in 1876. Working steam engines, an antique locomotive, domestic furnishings, and manufactured goods record U.S. technological accomplishments during the country's first century of existence. *900 Jefferson Drive, S.W. Facilities: Restrooms/ Telephone/Accessible by wheelchair*

The National Museum of American History expands the theme of American civilization in displays of domestic and political history, folk art, and a myriad technologies. Exhibits in this museum portray the cultural contributions to American life from various ethnic groups. Exhibits come alive with periodic demonstrations of musical instruments, spinning and weaving, printing presses, type casting, and early electrical experiments, among others. Some exhibits are expressly designed to be handled. The popular First Ladies' Hall displays gowns or other artifacts of every White House hostess from Martha Washington to the present. Although the hair styles on the mannekins are authentic, facial features are not. All mannekins' faces are identical. *Constitution Avenue between 12th and 14th Streets, N.W. Facilities: Restrooms/ Telephone/Cafeteria/Accessible by wheelchair*

The National Museum of Natural History portrays the world of nature. Perhaps the most popular exhibit is the legendary 45.5-carat blue Hope Diamond. In spite of its great beauty it is reputed to have brought bad luck to all its owners. Other popular exhibits are the dinosaurs, the blue whale, the largest African elephant on record, mummies, and dioramas illustrating habitat of wildlife and cultures of American Indians and Eskimos. The Insect Zoo delights adults as well as children. A living coral reef ecosystem intrigues scientists and visitors alike. *Constitution Avenue at 10th Street, N.W. Facilities: Restrooms/Telephone/Cafe/ Accessible by wheelchair*

The National Air and Space Museum traces the evolution of man's flight technology from early kites, gliders, and balloons to the primitive machine the Wright brothers first flew at Kitty Hawk in 1903, to artifacts of the latest explorations of outer space. *The Spirit of St. Louis,* which carried Charles Lindbergh on the first trans-Atlantic flight to Paris, hangs suspended along with other milestones of flight. Below them is the Apollo 11 command module, which returned three astronauts from the moon in 1969. Here you can touch a moon rock and examine the interior of the Skylab Orbital Workshop. You can vicariously experience the sensation of flight by watching special free cinemas on a giant screen, and you can visit the outer reaches of the universe by attending the planetarium show. *7th Street and Independence Avenue, N.W. Facilities: Restrooms/ Telephone/Cafeteria/Parking/ Accessible by wheelchair*

The Smithsonian's living museum—the National Zoological Park—is located 20 minutes from the Mall, in Rock Creek Park. The white tigers and the giant pandas are no doubt the zoo's most famous residents. The many other animals in the zoo live in spacious naturalistic outdoor surroundings. You can watch seals, otters, and polar bears cavort underwater; and you can walk among exotic birds in the bird house and the Great Flight Cage. *3001 Connecticut Avenue, N.W. Facilities: Restrooms/Telephone/ Cafe/Parking/Accessible by wheelchair*

THE ART GALLERIES

The regal marble National Gallery of Art contains extraordinary collections of the world's greatest masterpieces of Western art. It has an outstanding collection of Italian Renaissance art and splendid examples of every major school of art from the thirteenth century to the present.

In an incredibly generous gift to the nation, the National Gallery of Art was built with $15 million donated for that purpose by banker Andrew W. Mellon. He also donated his $30 million collection of 115 masterpieces and a $5 million endowment fund. Mellon's collection has been called "the greatest ever assembled by private hands." Beginning in 1927 Mellon started collecting the best examples of the greatest schools and periods of Western art expressly in order to found a national gallery of art. His collection included 21 exquisite masterpieces he had purchased from the Hermitage Gallery in Leningrad. Among this group was Raphael's "Alba Madonna," painted about 1510. It is considered one of the finest technical achievements in Renaissance painting, partly because of the successful composition within the difficult round framework.

Other outstanding collections have since been donated to the National Gallery, notably those of Joseph Widener, Samuel Kress, Lessing J. Rosenwald, and Chester Dale. In fact, all works in the gallery were donated or purchased with donated funds.

As acquisitions increased, more space was needed. So through the generosity of Paul Mellon, the late Ailsa Mellon Bruce, and the Andrew W. Mellon Foundation, the angular East Building was built to provide additional exhibition galleries. *Constitution Avenue at 6th Street, N.W. Facilities: Restrooms/Telephones/Cafe/Accessible by wheelchair*

Across the Mall, the circular Hirshhorn Museum and Sculpture Garden displays a collection of modern American and European painting and sculpture from the late nineteenth century to the present. They were donated by Joseph H. Hirshhorn, uranium magnate. *Independence Avenue at 8th Street, N.W. Facilities: Restrooms/Telephone/Cafe/Accessible by wheelchair*

The Freer Gallery of Art, located just west of the Castle, contains world-famous collections of Oriental, Near-Eastern, and Egyptian works of art donated by Charles Lang Freer, railroad car manufacturer. This gallery also contains American paintings by Winslow Homer, Albert Pinkham Ryder, and John Singer Sargent, and the world's most complete collection of works by James A. McNeill Whistler. A highlight of this collection is Whistler's opulent Peacock Room, created in oil color and gold on leather and wood especially to display one of his paintings. *12th Street and Jefferson Drive, S.W. Facilities: Restrooms/Telephones/Accessible by wheelchair*

Nearby, the Arthur M. Sackler Gallery of Asian Art and the National Museum of African Art display masterworks of Africa and Asia.

In downtown Washington, the magnificent old Patent Office Building contains the National Museum of American Art and the National Portrait Gallery. The National Museum specializes in American art from the eighteenth century to the present. The paintings of American Indians by George Catlin are especially interesting. Catlin spent six years in the early 1830s wandering throughout the wild western plains recording in his paintings the vanishing way of life of a doomed people—the Indians whom he so admired. The National Portrait Gallery is devoted to portraits of people who made significant contributions to American history, from the Indian princess Pocahontas to current national leaders. In this collection historic value is more important than artistic merit. *8th and G Streets, N.W. (Gallery Place Metro stop). Facilities: Restrooms/Telephone/Cafe/Accessible by wheelchair*

The Renwick Gallery, near the White House, specializes in contemporary and historic American decorative arts, crafts, and design. *17th Street and Pennsylvania Avenue, N.W. (2 blocks south of Farragut West Metro stop). Facilities: Restrooms/Telephone/Accessible by wheelchair*

The Corcoran Gallery of Art, near the Renwick, has a large collection of American and European painting and eighteenth century French decorative arts. *17th Street and New York Avenue, N.W. (4 blocks south of Farragut West Metro stop). Facilities: Restrooms/Telephone/Accessible by wheelchair*